D1625164

*more…*

"Searching for *God's* truth is stranger than fiction."
—Dottie, a searcher, Orlando, Florida

"I left my church after twelve years. I felt I needed to be in a church until I read your book and discovered it was not about going to church but being the church. And that is to be done everywhere I go and in everything I do."
—Ronda, mother and caregiver, Canby, Oregon

"Inside every one of us there is a Jake Colsen screaming to get out. Here you will find all the big questions about our struggle to live in the world by the Spirit, and some of the big answers, too."
—Rachael, nurse, Rugby, England

"This is not your typical Christian living book. I have never read anything like it before, but I certainly hope to again. I had my focus in the wrong place for a long time."
—Cory, IT specialist, Idaho

"Your book has put words and answers to the feelings and questions we have had along this journey."
—Michael, Prescott, Arizona

"This should be required reading for everyone. I can't say enough about how it changed me, and my relationship with the Lord."
—Pam, Indiana

"How could you know with such precision where we have come from, where we are, and what we are learning? You have put words to things deep in our hearts . . . too deep even to surface as thoughts, much less words."
—Maria Wade, wife and mother, Bloomington, Indiana

"This easy-to-read treatise on practical Christian thought and life points to the higher way of God's Son and Servant, Jesus. Jesus calls to tender hearts who choose to trust Him and walk with Him."
—Paul, handyman, Illinois

"I don't have the words to express how much I have been touched by this story. I'm glad to know that I'm not going crazy or being disloyal to feel as I do."                                —Beth, Tennessee

"It got me hooked right from the start and God used it to bring me closer to Him. Thank you for showing me that His body is not one congregation, denomination, or group of people, but that those He calls His own can be anyone, anywhere."
—Michelle, academic administrator,
Melbourne, Australia

"Your book is every conversation, thought, emotion, desire, and dream I have had for the past year. God really wants to wake up His church."
—Carole, single parent and massage therapist,
Shildon, United Kingdom

"It's better than any adventure movie I've ever seen!"
—Cynthia

"I received your book from a dear friend on Saturday. I couldn't put it down! I didn't go to work until I finished it! Something grand was lifted from me. Something I have been carrying around for fifty years."
—Jo-Anne, Realtor,
Kansas City, Missouri

"This is astounding! It sounds like the same journey I'm on but I grew tired of all the struggles. I want my relationship with my Father back."
—Matt, father of nine,
Kalispell, Montana

"These writings are more than a book. They are a living two-edged sword, God revealing Himself in the midst of hungry souls that have attended church, only to find ourselves very needy and empty."
—Joyce, Rochester, New York

*more...*

"This book will cut through all the red tape of 'religion.' It will free you from yourself and allow you to believe and accept the love God has for you."                    —Cathey, sister, Florida

"It is exactly what I am looking for in confirming what God has started in me."                    —Chris, missionary, France

"I am spellbound!"                    —Judy

"Little did I know that this book so far would be the catalyst to finally lay it all down. At first I thought this was going to be an antichurch book and I found out that it is *so prochurch*! *How could I not see these things before?*"
                    —Patricia, Massachusetts

"What a great read! This book really speaks to some issues that I have been struggling with over the past few years."
                    —Bill, missionary, Wales

"I recommended this book to a friend as one of the best writings I have seen on practical Christian thinking. She wrote back to me that she could not stop reading it once she began, and afterwards she felt that she had been born again—*again*!"                    —Paul

"To say I enjoyed it and was encouraged would be an understatement."          —Brett, consultant, Durban, South Africa

"You express so clearly my concern and hope for Christ's church today."                    —Richard, Alabama

"I was so compelled that I had to read through it in two days. I am absolutely speechless, also so excited at the same time—so many things confirmed and many truths learned."
                    —Lysle, former pastor, England

"This is the best story with resounding truths that I have ever read. A huge weight has been lifted off my shoulders."
                    —Kristopher, Texas

"It is so refreshing, sobering, and exciting to read such freeing words devoid of any manipulation or legalism."

—Nick, Australia

"This book is a healing balm and I could not quit reading it until I had read it all. So much wonderful truth here and so simply stated."

—Margie, Washington

"Thank you, from an almost-ready-to-give-up-being-a-Christian because nothing seemed to make much sense anymore and there was no life in my supposed 'life' in Christ."          —Colleen

"*I am flabbergasted!* So are my husband and best friend. I am personally so excited to have the *verbiage* to express what God has been speaking to me for years. Everything you say is bang on! I feel like the weight of the world has been lifted off of me."

—Gay

"Thanks for the beautiful and powerful story. Your writing really brought me closer to our awesome God and Father."

—Rudolf, The Netherlands

"I can't even begin to express what this work means for me. I'm beginning to see that everything I do can be done out of love for the Father and others and that obligation can be replaced."

—Jeremy

"I'm totally hooked!"          —Michelle, Australia

"What I have read has blown me away completely. I can't seem to get my mind around the point that *all* of the answers that John is giving seem to be those which I have been having, on those rare occasions when I seem to hear what the Holy Spirit is saying. And they have been the ones that I have been inclined to disregard as my imagination."          —Denis, Australia

Other Books by WAYNE JACOBSEN

*Authentic Relationships* (with Clay Jacobsen)
*He Loves Me*
*In My Father's Vineyard*
*Tales of the Vine*
*The Shack* (in collaboration with author
Wm. Paul Young)

# SO YOU DON'T WANT TO GO TO CHURCH ANYMORE

## An Unexpected Journey

*Wayne Jacobsen and Dave Coleman*

**windblown**
MEDIA
*Los Angeles, California*

SO YOU DON'T WANT
TO GO TO CHURCH ANYMORE

Published by:

Windblown Media
4680 Calle Norte • Newbury Park, CA 91320
(805) 498-2484
www.windblownmedia.com

Published in association with Hachette Book Group USA.

Except where otherwise indicated, all Scripture quotations are from the Holy Bible, New International Version. Copyright © 1973, 1978, 1984 by the International Bible Society. Used by permission of Zondervan Bible Publishers.

Scriptures noted NLT are taken from the *Holy Bible*, New Living Translation, copyright © 1996, 2004. Used by permission of Tyndale House Publishers, Inc., Carol Stream, Illinois 60188. All rights reserved.

ISBN-13: 978-1-60751-334-6

Printed in the United States of America

*Cover design courtesy of MercyArts Studio (mercyarts@sbcglobal.net)*

*Dedication*

---

To the Blessed Ones—
those today and
throughout history
who have been insulted,
excluded, and lied about
for simply following the
Lamb beyond the accepted norms
of tradition and culture.

(See MATTHEW 5:11)

#  Contents

# Acknowledgments

The crafting of this book has been a four-year journey, where we have posted the rough draft of each chapter in succession online. We had hoped to complete it in a year, but it took us four. So, we most want to thank our patient readers who endured this experiment with us, encouraged us with their comments, and added to this content with their own stories and questions.

We've also had some marvelous people read and proof the manuscript for us. Canadians Bruce and Judy Woodford worked through every chapter with us, proofreading for our mistakes and adding their ideas. In this printing we added other editors to help shape this manuscript: Kate Lapin, Julie Williams, Paul Hayden, and Mitch Disney. Thanks to you all. If any mistakes survived their proofing, it was probably due to Wayne's irresistible urge to tweak the manuscript until the last possible second.

Our cover design was graciously provided out of the clear blue by Stephen at MercyArts Studio in Chicago, Illinois, with help from Dave Aldrich of Rhode Island.

We also want to thank our wives for their outrageous support and encouragement in this project and the many brothers and sisters who have helped show us "a more excellent way."

# Stranger and Stranger Still

At that moment he was the last person I wanted to see. My day had been bad enough already; now I was certain it was about to get worse.

Yet there he was. A moment before he had poked his head into the cafeteria, walked over to the beverage station, and poured himself some fruit juice. I thought about ducking under the table but quickly realized I was too old for that. Maybe he wouldn't see me back in the corner. I looked down and covered my face with my hands.

Out of the cracks between my fingers, I could see he had turned, leaned back against the counter, and took a drink while surveying the room. Then he squinted toward me as he realized he wasn't alone and with a surprised look he started toward me. Of all nights, why here? Why now?

It had been our worst day ever in a long and torturous battle. Since three o'clock that afternoon, when the asthma made its first attempt that day to strangle Andrea, our twelve-year-old daughter, we had been on guard for her life. First we rushed her to the hospital watching her struggle for every breath. Then we watched as the doctors and nurses battled with her asthma for the use of her lungs.

I admit I do not deal with this well, although you'd think I would with all the practice I've had. My wife and I have watched our daughter suffer all of her life, never certain when a sudden, life-threatening attack would send us scurrying to the hospital. It makes me so angry to watch her suffer; no matter how much we've prayed for her and had others do the same, the asthma continues to get worse.

A couple of hours before, the medication had finally kicked in and she began to breathe more easily. My wife headed home to get some much-needed sleep and relieve her parents, who'd come to be with our other daughter. I stayed the night. Andrea finally fell asleep and I found my way to the cafeteria for something to drink and a quiet place to read. I was too wired to sleep.

Grateful to find the place deserted, I poured myself a cup of coffee and sat down in the shadows of a distant corner. I was so angry I couldn't even think straight. *What have I done so wrong that my daughter must suffer like this? Why does God ignore my desperate pleas for her healing?* Other parents gripe about playing taxicab for all their children's activities; I don't even know if Andrea will survive her next asthma attack, and I worry that the steroids she's on will stunt her growth.

Somewhere in the middle of a good wallow in my anger, he poked his head into my private sanctuary. Now he was walking over to my table and I honestly thought about punching him in the mouth if he dared to open it. Deep down, though, I knew I wouldn't. I'm violent only on the inside, not on the outside where anyone else can see it.

I've never met anyone more frustrating than John. I was so excited when we first met, and honestly I've never met anyone as wise as he. But he's brought me nothing but grief. Since he's come into my life, I've lost my lifelong dream job, been ostracized from the church I'd helped to start fifteen years before, and even found my marriage in rougher waters than I'd ever known.

To understand just how frustrated I am, you would have to come back with me to the day I first met John. As incredible as the beginning was, it doesn't compare to all we've been through since.

My wife and I celebrated our seventeenth wedding anniversary by taking a three-day trip to Pismo Beach on the central California coast. On our way home on Saturday, we stopped in downtown San Luis Obispo for lunch and shopping. Its revitalized downtown is a major draw for the area and on this sunny April day the streets were jammed.

After lunch we split up since our preferred browsing places are quite different. I went to loiter in the bookstores while she trolled the clothing stores and gift shops. Finishing before our scheduled rendezvous time, I had perched myself against the wall of a store while enjoying a chocolate ice-cream cone.

I couldn't help but notice the heated argument going on a few feet up the street in front of The Gap. Four college-aged students and two middle-aged men were holding bright blue handbills and gesturing wildly. I had seen the handbills earlier, tucked under windshield wipers and lying scattered in the gutter. It was an invitation to a play about the flames of hell that was being produced at a local church.

"Who'd want to go to this second-rate production?"

"I'll never set foot in a church again!"

"The only thing I learned in church was how to feel guilty!"

"Been there, done that, got the scars, and ain't going back!"

In the few moments since I had begun eavesdropping, I think every one of them threw in a comment. Another would jump in as if he was going to burst from the pressure if he couldn't add their own venom.

"Where do these arrogant people get off thinking they can judge me?"

"I'd like to know what Jesus would think if he walked into one of these churches today!"

"I don't think he'd go."

"And if he did, he'd probably fall asleep."

Laughter drowned him out.

"Or maybe he'd die laughing."

"Or crying," another voice offered, which caused everyone to pause and think a moment.

"Do you think he'd wear a suit?"

"Only to hide the whip he'd sneak in to do a little house-cleaning."

The increasing volume drew the attention of those passing by. Their pace would slow as they were drawn into the commotion. Some drawn by the passion and intrigued by the assault on something as sacred as religion joined in like puppies at the food bowl. Still others hung around on the fringes to listen. Some even asked me what was going on.

Then a full-fledged argument developed as some of the newcomers challenged the antichurch cynics. Accusations volleyed quickly in the crowd. Most of them I had heard before: complaints about extravagant facilities, hypocrites, boring sermons, always asking for money, and burnout from too many meetings. Those who sought to defend the church had to admit some of these weaknesses but tried to point out many good things churches have done.

That's when I noticed him. He could have been anywhere from late thirties to early fifties. It was difficult to tell. He was short, perhaps only five foot four with dark, wavy hair and an unkempt beard. Both were peppered with streaks of gray. Wearing a faded green sweatshirt, jeans, and running shoes, he had a rugged look that made me wonder if he was a holdover from the rebellious sixties—except that he wasn't shuffling by aimlessly.

In fact, what had caught my eye was the determined purpose of his gait, moving directly toward the growing debate. His face was as intense as a German shepherd when it's pursuing an unfamiliar sound in the night. He seemed to melt into the crowd and then emerged in the center of it, surveying the more vocal ones. When his eyes turned in my direction, I was captured by their intensity. They were deep—and alive! I was riveted. He seemed to know something no one else did.

By this time the debate had turned hostile. Those who had attacked the church had turned their anger toward Jesus himself, mocking him as an impostor. As intended, that only made the churchgoers in the group more livid. "Wait until you have to look in his face as you sink into hell!" one said. I thought the combatants were going to start swinging at one another when the stranger floated his question into the crowd.

"You really have no idea what Jesus was like, do you?"

The words slipped off the man's lips as gently as the breeze wafted through the trees overhead. They were in stark contrast to the heated argument that swirled around him. They were so softly spoken that I read them on his lips more than heard them. But their impact was not lost on the crowd. The noisy clamor subsided quickly as tension-filled faces gave way to puzzled expressions. *Who said that?* was the unspoken question that filled the eyes of their surprised faces as they scanned the others around them.

I chuckled under my breath because no one was looking at the man who had just spoken. For one thing, he was so short that it was easy to pass over him. But, intrigued by his demeanor, I had been watching him and the crowd for the last few moments.

As people were glancing around, he spoke again into the stunned silence. "Do you have any idea what he was like?"

This time all eyes turned downward toward the voice and were surprised to see the man who'd spoken.

"What do you know about it, old man?" one of them finally asked, his mockery dripping off each word until the disapproving gaze of the crowd silenced him. He laughed it off and looked away, embarrassed, grateful that their eyes had swung back to the stranger. But the stranger was in no hurry to speak. The resulting silence hung in the air, far beyond the point of awkwardness. A few nervous glances and shrugs shot through the crowd, but no one spoke and no one left. During this time the man scanned the crowd pausing to hold each person's gaze for a brief second. When he caught my eye, everything inside seemed to melt. I looked away instantly. After a few moments I glanced back, hoping he was no longer looking in my direction.

After what seemed an insufferably long time, he spoke again. His first words were whispered directly to the man who had threatened the others with hell. "You really have no idea what motivates you, do you?" His tone was one of sorrow, and his words sounded like an invitation. There was not a trace of anger in them. Embarrassed, the man threw his hands up and rolled his eyes as if he didn't understand the question.

The stranger let him twist in the gaze of the crowd briefly, then, looking around the circle, he began to speak again, his words flowing softly. "He was nothing special to look at. He could walk down this street today and not one of you would even notice him. In fact, he had the kind of face you would shy away from, certain he wouldn't fit in with your crowd.

"But he was as gentle a man as one would ever know. He could silence detractors without ever raising his voice. He never bullied, never drew attention to himself, nor did he ever pretend to like what vexed his soul. He was real, to the very core.

"And at the core of that being was love." The stranger paused and shook his head. "Wow! Did he love!" His eyes looked far past the crowd now, seeming to peer across the depths of time and space. "We didn't even know what love was, until we saw it in him. It was everyone, too, even those who hated him. He still cared for them, hoping somehow they would find a way out of their self-inflicted souls to recognize who stood among them.

"And with all that love, he was completely honest. Yet even when his actions or words exposed people's darkest motives, they didn't feel shamed. They felt safe, really safe with him. His words conveyed not even a hint of judgment, simply an entreaty to come to God. There was no one you would trust more quickly with your deepest secrets. If someone was going to catch you at your worst moment, you'd want it to be him.

"He wasted no time mocking others, nor their religious trappings." He glanced at those who had just done so. "If he had something to say to them, he'd say it and move on and you would know you'd been loved more than ever before." Here the man stopped, his eyes closed and mouth clenched as if choking back tears that would melt him in an instant if he gave in to them.

"I'm not talking about mamby-pamby sentimentalism, either. He loved, really loved. It didn't matter if you were Pharisee or prostitute, disciple or blind beggar, Jew, Samaritan, or Gentile. His love held itself out for any to embrace. Most did, too, when they saw him. Though so few ended up following him, for the few moments his presence passed by them, they tasted a freshness and power they could never deny even years later. Somehow he seemed to know everything about them but loved them deeply all the same."

He paused and scanned the crowd. In the last couple of moments perhaps as many as thirty more people had stopped to listen, their gaze firmly on the man and their mouths agape in bewilderment. I can record his words here but am bereft of an adequate description of their impact. No one within earshot could deny their power or their authenticity. They rang from the very depths of his soul.

"And when he hung there from that filthy cross"—the man's eyes looked up into the trees that towered over us—"that love still poured down—on mocker and disillusioned friend alike. As he approached the dark chamber of death, wearied of the torture and feeling separated from his Father, he continued to drink from the cup that would finally consume our self-will and shame. There was no finer moment in all of human history. His anguish became the conduit for his life to be shared with us. This was no madman. This was God's Son, poured out to the last breath, to open full and free access for you to his Father."

As he spoke further, I was struck by the intimacy of his words. He talked like someone who had been with him. In fact, I remember thinking, *This man is exactly how I would picture John the Disciple to be.*

No sooner had the thought crossed my mind than he stopped midsentence. Turning to his right, his eyes seemed to seek something in the crowd. Suddenly his eyes locked on mine. The hair on the back of my neck stood up and my body quivered with a wave of chills. He held my gaze for a moment; then a brief but certain smile spread over his lips as he winked and nodded at me.

At least that's the way I remember it now. I was shocked at the time. *Is he acknowledging my thought? That would be silly. Even if he were John, he wouldn't be a mind reader. What am I thinking? How could he be a two-thousand-year-old disciple? It's just not possible.*

As he turned away, I glanced behind me to see if anyone else could have been the target of his gaze. It didn't look that way, and no one around me seemed to take notice of his wink and smile. I was stunned, feeling as if I'd just been hit in the head with an errant football. Electricity raked over my body as questions raced through my mind. I had to find out more about this stranger.

The crowd was swelling in size as more and more people poked their heads in, trying to figure out what was going on. Even the stranger seemed to grow increasingly uncomfortable with the spectacle the scene was quickly becoming.

"If I were you," he said with a wink and a smile as his eyes swept over those who'd started the discussion, "I would waste far less time ragging on religion and find out just how much Jesus wants to be your friend without any strings attached. He will care for you and, if given a chance, will become more real to you than your best friend. You will cherish him more than anything else you desire. He will give you a purpose and a fullness of life that will carry you through every stress and pain and will change you from the inside to show you what true freedom and joy really are."

With that he turned and made his way through the crowd in the opposite direction from where I was standing. No one moved or said anything for a moment, unsure just how to end the confrontation and break up.

I tried to move through the crowd so that I could talk to this man personally. Could he really have been John? If not, who was he? How did he know the things he seemed to speak about so confidently?

It was difficult to navigate through the pack of people and keep my eye on John. I pushed my way through just in time to see him turn down a gap between two buildings. He was headed up Bubble Gum Alley, a forty-yard stretch of brick wall that joined the shopping district with a parking lot behind. It had gotten its name from the thousands of chewed-up wads of gum that had been affixed to the wall during the years. The array of colors made for an impressive if somewhat grotesque sight.

He was only fifteen feet in front of me when he went out of sight. I was relieved to know I'd at least get a chance to talk with him, for no one else had pursued him. I rounded the corner, prepared to call out for him to stop, but instead stopped instantly upon looking down the alley.

It was empty. I turned back to the street confused. Had he really turned in there? I looked both directions up the sidewalk but didn't see any green sweatshirts like the one he was wearing. No, he did go in there. I was certain of it. But he could not have covered the forty yards in the three seconds it had taken me to get to the alley.

My heart began to race. Fearful I would miss him. In a panic I finally ran down the alley past the brightly colored wads of gum. There was no doorway or nook where he could have gone. At the end I burst into the parking lot, scanning every direction at once. Nothing. A few people were getting out of their cars, but no sign of the stranger.

Confused, I ran back up the alley and into the street, surveying quickly for any green sweatshirts, all the time praying that I could find him again. I looked in nearby store windows and at passing cars, but to no avail. He was gone. I could have kicked myself for not having followed him more closely.

I finally sat down on a bench, a bit disoriented by the whole experience. I massaged my bowed forehead, trying to pull together a cohesive thought. I could hardly finish a sentence in my mind before another thought would intrude. Who was he, and what happened to him? His words had touched the deepest hungers of my heart and the thought of his wink at me still gave me the shivers.

I knew I'd never see him again and wrote off the whole morning as one of those inexplicable events in life that would never make any sense.

I couldn't have been more wrong.

- 2 -

# A Walk in the Park

A thousand times in the weeks that followed I replayed the events of that morning in my mind—reconstructing the man's words and my thoughts. The thought that he reminded me of John the Apostle had been a passing fancy, except that he seemed to acknowledge it with his penetrating wink.

But how could John still be alive after two thousand years? Could it have been a miraculous appearance, as when Moses and Elijah were transfigured in Jesus' presence? Even if he was alive, could he have read my mind or disappeared so easily from view?

I even went back and reread Jesus' puzzling words to Peter about John's future. He had just warned Peter that the day would come when men would lead Peter to his death because of his friendship with Christ. Disturbed by the thought, and perhaps desiring not to go that way alone, Peter pointed to John and asked about his future. Jesus' answer shocked everyone. "If I want him to remain alive until I return, what is that to you? You must follow me."

John wrote that Jesus' words had started a rumor among the other disciples that John would not die. But he went on to say that was not exactly what Jesus had said. Obviously the larger lesson of Jesus' words was for Peter to follow the path the Lord laid out for him and without comparing himself to others. A worthy lesson, no doubt, but did Jesus mean anything more by that illustration?

I second-guessed everything about that morning. It didn't help that when I told the story to my wife and one other close friend they hummed the theme music from *The Twilight Zone* and laughed it off. Their refusal to take me seriously made me far less certain of what had actually happened that day. What I could not deny, however, was that whoever that man was, his words had shaken me to the core of my Christianity.

I had never heard anyone talk about Jesus the way he did, and he had provoked an insatiable hunger within me to find out more about this Jesus I thought I knew. Over the next few weeks I read all of the Gospels again—this time looking beyond the lessons Jesus taught to see just what kind of person he was. I realized that although I had been a Christian for more than two decades, I had no concept of who Jesus was as a person and no idea how I could change that. The harder I tried, the more frustrated I became. I threw myself headlong into my ministry, hoping to bury the hunger and the questions that the stranger had triggered.

Four and a half months after that initial encounter, things were about to get even stranger. I had set apart one morning to study for an infrequent opportunity to teach in our Sunday morning services, but a series of crises prevented me from ever opening my books. First, the volunteer sound tech had a chance to go out of town and would not be there on Sunday. Could I find a replacement? Someone else stopped by who wanted to complain about how unfriendly our church was. She had been attending for two years and had not once been invited out by anyone.

Then Ben and Marsha Hopkins came by to tell me they wouldn't be at home group that night. This was the third time in a row they were going to miss, not a good example for someone who was my assistant leader. When I pressed them, they finally told me that they weren't happy with the church and were considering leaving. I tried to talk them out of it. I'd invested countless hours getting them ready to lead a home group on their own—how could they leave now?

"Our children are enjoying a youth group at another church closer to our home and we've been uncomfortable for some time with how impersonal this church has become." When they first came, they were almost ready for a divorce. I had spent hours with them helping them rekindle their marriage. Now just as they were getting to a place where they could give something back, they were running off to greener pastures.

Then finally, to top it all off, the pastor called right after lunch to cancel a meeting he had asked me to schedule with two of our elders who had some concerns about our building program. He said he just didn't feel like dealing with it that day. It had taken three weeks for me to arrange that meeting. I was furious and had to get out for some fresh air.

My office door betrayed my frustration to the rest of the office as it slammed shut harder than I intended. It startled my secretary and drew looks from down the hallway. I motioned back to the door, exasperated, as if it had made all that noise on its own. As I looked back my eyes fixed on the ever-familiar sign: *Jake Colsen, Associate Pastor.*

I still remember the first day I walked through that door, surprised that the nameplate was already in place and awed by the responsibility it placed on my shoulders. I had never planned to enter full-time ministry, but the day I walked through that door I felt all my dreams had finally been fulfilled. Four years later those dreams proved as elusive as ever.

The son of working-class parents, I had grown up in church. Even through the tempestuous teenage years of the early seventies I never strayed far from my spiritual roots. Graduating from college in 1979 with a business degree, I ended up handling commercial real estate in Kingston, California, a sprawling metropolis in the fertile farmland of central California. The economy had exploded in the eighties and early nineties and I had built a lucrative practice and a stellar reputation.

My wife and I had helped found the congregation I now worked for. Fifteen years earlier a few families and some college students, disillusioned by the power games being played in the traditional church we attended, decided we'd do better starting a new one. We met in homes for a while, treasuring the fellowship we had together, but soon rented a building and hung out our shingle for the community. In the early days growth had been slow, but in the last ten years we'd grown to more than two thousand members, constructed our own building, and had a full complement of pastoral staff.

Imagine how flattered I was when the pastor invited me to join that staff to oversee the business affairs and to help with pastoral care. I was thirty-nine at the time, very comfortable in my profession and raising two young children. The adult Sunday school class I taught was one of the most popular on the schedule and I'd just completed two terms on the church board.

He told me how much I was needed, that I could free him from responsibilities he wasn't gifted to meet. Even though I was making more than enough money in real estate, I knew it was just money—the "god of mammon," as I'd heard it preached. Was I wasting my life on my own pleasures? What did my life really count for? I rarely had time for the things I thought most important, so I took the job, hoping I could finally put that nagging guilt to rest.

And it did for a while. For the first year or two, I was caught up in the importance of being on staff at a growing church and actually having time to pray and study the Bible. Soon, however, the workload became oppressive. I not only worked full days but was out five or six nights a week. I didn't even have time to dabble in real estate on the side as I had planned to help offset my lower paycheck.

When my frustration peaked, I often sought solace in a long

walk. I would tell my secretary I'd be out for a while and leave the ministry complex for a park two blocks away. It had often been my refuge and sometimes prayer closet, though I hadn't been out there much in the oppressively hot months of the Central Valley summer. Today it was in the lower eighties—a sign that summer would eventually pass and the cooler days of autumn were approaching.

Turning the corner, however, I was surprised to see the park filled with children—until I remembered that my wife had said it was going to be a minimum school day for our kids. Disappointed, I scanned the park to see if there were any quiet corners I could stake out. That's when I noticed him—a lone figure on one of the benches across the park. Even from this distance he looked like the stranger I'd seen in San Luis Obispo.

My heart skipped a beat. I had often prayed God would give me an opportunity to talk to that man, but I had given up any hope of that. The thought of him brought back incredible memories of that morning and the hunger it had tapped in my heart. I was almost certain it couldn't be him, but I thought I'd at least take a closer look while I was there.

As I approached him, he appeared to be the right height, but that was tough to judge since he was sitting down. The build and beard looked similar, but he had on sunglasses and a baseball cap that made it hard to be certain. He seemed to be staring off in the distance, unaware of my approach.

I couldn't take my eyes off him, and my heart was pounding wildly.

*What if this is him?*

*What should I do?*

As I walked past him, his head turned and I immediately averted my eyes. *It can't be him.* I couldn't decide. I didn't have any idea what to say and had dawdled about as long as I could without saying something to him, so I moved on down the sidewalk. I was ten yards past when I had enough courage to pause briefly and pretend to scan the park as an excuse to let my eyes run back to the man on the bench.

It certainly looked like him.

His head started to turn and I turned away again, feeling awkward. Before I knew it I was walking away from him again. Fifty yards up was another empty bench. I meandered to it and sat down, able then to look back. The man was just getting up from the bench and started off in the opposite direction.

*Oh, no! What do I do? I guess it's now or never.*

I jumped up from the bench and started after him, catching up a few feet with every step. Finally I was close enough that I either had to pass him by again or speak. "Excuse me, sir!" The words popped out of my lips before I knew for sure they were coming.

He stopped and turned toward me. "Yes?" One syllable was a lousy sample, but the voice sounded close.

"This may sound funny, but you look like somebody I saw a few months ago on the coast in downtown San Luis Obispo. Any chance it was you?" His sunglasses hid any expression. If I could just see his eyes, I'd know for sure.

"As a matter of fact, I was over there a few months ago, but only for a few days. Did we meet?"

"No, but someone who looked like you broke into an argument some people were having in the downtown district."

"It could have been me," he answered, shrugging his shoulders.

"This was an argument about religion. And if you're the same man, you stepped into the debate and spoke about Jesus and how much he really loved people. Does this make any sense?"

"It does. I talk to people all the time, especially those who are seeking spiritual things."

"My name is Jake Colsen." I stuck out my hand to shake his.

"Hi, Jake. I'm John," he responded, offering his hand as well.

The next breath didn't come easily—neither did the next few words. I felt as if I'd lost my breath to a stomach punch. "Are you the same man who spoke to those people? It was a Saturday morning. Did you see me there?"

"I don't specifically recall your being there, but it sounds like the kind of conversation I often find myself in."

"Could we talk for a moment?" I glanced at my watch, realizing I had only thirty minutes before an appointment back at the office. I motioned toward the bench not far away.

"I'd be delighted."

We walked over and sat down, both of us gazing out across the park.

"This is going to sound strange," I finally began, "but I have been praying for the chance to meet you. Your words really touched me that day. You spoke about Jesus as if you had been with him personally. At one point I even wondered if you were John the Apostle."

He chuckled. "That would make me a bit old, wouldn't it?"

"I know this sounds crazy, but as I had that thought you stopped in midsentence, turned toward me, and nodded as if you were agreeing with me. I tried to chase you down as you left the group, but I seemed to lose you in the crowd."

"Perhaps it wasn't meant to be then. At least we're here now. What did you want to talk about?"

"Are you?"

"Am I what?"

"Are you John?"

"John, the disciple of Jesus?" He smiled, obviously amused at the prospect. "Well, you already know my name is John, and I do claim to be a disciple of his."

"But are you *the* John?"

"Why is that so important to you?"

"If you are, I've got some things I want to ask you."

"And if I'm not?"

I didn't know what to say. I had been deeply affected by his words—whoever he was. He seemed to know some things about Jesus that had certainly escaped me. "I'd want to talk to you anyway, I guess."

"Why?"

"Your words in San Luis Obispo moved me deeply. You seem to know Jesus in a way I'd only hoped to. I'm a pastor, on staff at a church in town—City Center Fellowship. Ever hear of it?"

"No, I don't think so!" He shook his head.

His answer offended me a little. Why wouldn't he know about us? "Do you live around here?"

"No. Actually this is the first time I have been to Kingston."

"Really? What brings you here?"

"Maybe your prayers," he said, laughing. "I'm not really sure."

"Listen, I've got to go in a few minutes. Could we meet again sometime?"

"I don't know. I really don't have the freedom to commit to an appointment. If we need to get together again, I'm sure we will. This happened without a schedule."

"Could you come over for dinner tonight? We could talk then."

"No, I'm sorry. I already have something tonight. What's going on?"

Where to start? I had so much to ask but only twenty minutes left before I had to rush back to the office, and even then I'd be late.

"I am really frustrated. It seems like everyone I've talked to lately is running on empty—even Christians I've known for decades. I met with one of our elders yesterday, who I've always thought to be a rock. Davis is pretty disillusioned with it all these days. He told me he often wonders if God is even real or if this whole Christianity thing is just a crock."

"What did you tell him?"

"I tried to encourage him. I told him we couldn't live by sight but by faith; that he's done a lot of wonderful things for God and he'll honor that someday. We just have to be faithful and not trust our feelings."

"So you told him he didn't have the right to his feelings, or his questions?"

"No, that's not what I said."

"Are you sure?" The question was gentle, not accusing.

Taken back, I replayed what I had said to him.

"Understand something, Jake, this life in Jesus is a real thing. It's not a game. When people sense something's wrong, you know what I've discovered? Something usually is."

"And I told him to ignore it." I said the words more to myself than to John. I shook my head at the realization.

"Do you think you helped him?"

"I don't know. I gave him a lot of encouragement. He seemed to be better."

John didn't speak, letting me think it through.

"You're right, I didn't help him at all. I guess I just blamed him."

"Do you think he'll come back to you next time he has those thoughts?"

I just shook my head, regretting almost everything I'd told him that morning. "I'll have to call him back and try again."

"But what about you, Jake? Is it working for you?"

"Is what working?"

"Your faith. Are you experiencing God's life to the degree you desire it?"

"I get frustrated from time to time, just like today. But overall I can't think of anything I'd rather do than what I'm doing right now."

John's head didn't move.

"I mean, I miss the money, and the free time I had, but this is far more worthwhile. We're making a big impact on this city."

Again he sat silently. I didn't know what else to say, but before I knew it tears began to well up in my eyes and I found myself gasping for breath. Suddenly I felt incredibly alone.

John's head finally turned my way. "I'm not talking about what you're doing. Are you filled with the love of Jesus like you were the first day you believed in him?"

The words worked their way down into my soul and I felt my insides melting like a pat of butter in a hot pan.

"N . . . N . . . N . . . No!" I couldn't seem to get it out, my voice jerking with small intakes of air. When the word finally came out, it was accompanied by a long guttural sigh. "That hasn't worked in years. It seems like the more I do for God, the further he gets away from me."

"Or, perhaps the further you get from him."

"What?" Whoever he was, he certainly looked at everything from a different angle.

"Do you know why you feel so empty?"

"I haven't really thought about it, John. I've been busy and it seems like he's using me to touch people. I just figured this is the way it was supposed to be. I don't let myself think about it too much. It's too discouraging. I mean, I have a lot to be thankful for—a loving and understanding wife, wonderful children, a nice home. And I'm serving God with everything I have. But it's hollow in here." I punched my fist against my chest as my eyes moistened even more.

"Davis scared you, didn't he?"

"Huh?" For the second time I was thrown off track.

"Maybe you feel just as empty as he does, but you won't slow down enough to admit it."

"I would never have thought of that, but I do remember how uncomfortable I felt when he was talking. He was asking questions I didn't want to answer."

"You know what this whole thing is about, Jake?" John leaned back on the bench, crossed his arms over his chest, and looked out across the playground. "It's about life—God's real life filling your own. He moves in so that you will no longer entertain any doubts about his reality. It's the kind of relationship that Adam tasted when he walked in the garden with God and heard his great plan to have a people through whom he could demonstrate his reality to the world in more ways than you could ever imagine. It is the kind of life Jesus lived that was more than sufficient to meet every need he faced, from feeding multitudes with a little boy's lunch to healing a sick woman who touched the hem of his robe. This life is not some philosophical thought you can conjure up through meditation or some kind of theological abstraction to be debated. It is fullness. It is freedom. It is joy and peace no matter what happens—even if your doctor uses the C-word when he gives you the results of your MRI. This is the kind of life that he came to share with everyone who will give up trying to control his own life and embrace his agenda.

"His agenda is certainly not what so many have come to believe, like our working hard, building big ministries or new buildings. It's about life that you can see, taste, and touch—something you can frolic in every day that you live. I know my words fail to describe it adequately, but you know what I'm talking about. You've had moments like that, haven't you?"

"Yes. Yes, I have, but they were always so fleeting. I remember how much it was like that in the early days, but I'm a long ways from that now. What's wrong with me? How can I be a Christian for so long, be so active in the church, and still not get it? How did I lose touch with that life? I certainly was not trying to."

"I've watched it happen again and again," John replied. "It

is epidemic today. Somehow our spiritual experience makes the wrong things important and we end up distracted from his true life. It happened in the early church, too. Do you remember what happened in Ephesus and what Jesus said to them in the Revelation letter? Their theology was impeccable. They knew the truth so well they could spot error like a fly in a bowl of soup at a hundred paces. They were not afraid to confront those who put themselves forward in ministry to find out who was telling the truth and who was fabricating a message just to build names for themselves. Their endurance in times of suffering was second to none in all Christendom. Suffering seemed to make them stronger the longer they faced it, and they never complained when assailed by others. But for all that, was Jesus pleased with them?"

I had recently taught that passage, so I knew what John was talking about. "No, he chided them for having left their first love."

"That's right. Amazing, isn't it? What they lacked created such a vacuum that any good they might have accomplished was swallowed up by it. They had left the ravishing love they had for Jesus in the beginning. Without it, their service was meaningless. You can get so busy working for him that you lose sight of knowing him. Too little of it was motivated by their love for him or his for them. That made everything else they did not just worthless, but destructive actually."

"That's me!" I said. "You are talking about me."

"It's an old story, Jake. It's been rerun a million times under a million different names. Do you remember the day the love of Jesus first captured your heart?"

The memories came flooding back. "Yes. I was in junior high school, only twelve or thirteen at the time, but I knew something was up. My parents were in the other room praying with thirty or so other people. They'd been at it for four hours with no sign of letting up. What's more, they were enjoying it. It was the same thing every Friday night. They couldn't wait to get together and pray. Sometimes they sang, sometimes they laughed, and sometimes they even cried. They rarely broke up before eleven and often went far longer.

"This was quite a change for my parents, who had grown up in church. We were third-generation Baptist on my father's side and Presbyterian on my mother's. My parents had settled in as active members of the Baptist church—attending regularly and serving on a multitude of committees. But they never seemed to enjoy church. Some mornings we could even talk them out of going.

"But this was different. We couldn't drag them away with a tow truck. They had moved from being mere church attendees to people passionate about their walk with God. In the process God was changing their lives. Old habits fell away, God's presence was stronger than their needs, and they were reading the Bible at every opportunity. I remember them praying about everything. They were joyful, free, and alive in their faith for the first time. It made us kids hungry for it as well. They prayed for us and that's the first time I remember knowing the life of God. I even remember hearing God's voice for the first time."

"What happened to your parents' spiritual hunger?"

"For a few years it grew, and they wanted their church to embrace it as well. But suspicions abounded and accusations flew. When the dust settled some months later, it was clear that they were no longer welcome at the church. They resigned their membership, but it didn't dampen their zeal. They just saw it as persecution.

"Since they were no longer welcome at their church, they decided to start a new one together with the people they prayed with. The first gathering brought more than eighty people, and they crammed into a small house. The atmosphere was electric. They decided to get organized, rent a building, and hire a pastor."

"Strange, isn't it, that forming something into what they thought was a church could do what persecution couldn't? There is nothing the Father desires for you more than that you fall squarely in the lap of his love and never move from that place for the rest of your life. God's plan from the days of Creation to the day of the Second Coming was designed to bring people into the relationship of love that the Father, Son, and Spirit have shared for eternity. He wants nothing less—and nothing else!

"This is no distant God who sent his Son with a list of rules to follow or rituals to practice. His mission was to invite us into his love—into a relationship with God the Father that Jesus described as friendship. But what do we do? We are so quickly captured by a work-driven religious culture that thrives on guilt, conformity, and manipulation that it devours the very love it seeks to sustain.

"In Ephesus it was ferreting out false teachers. In Galatia it was getting everyone to observe the Old Testament rituals. Today it's convincing people to cooperate with the church program. It doesn't matter what leads people away from God's life. Anything will do, as long as it preoccupies them enough to serve as an adequate substitute for the real thing. It's easier to see the problem when the standard is circumcision in Ephesus than when it is Sunday morning attendance in Kingston. But both can lead to the same thing: bored and disillusioned believers, no longer embracing Father's life."

I didn't know what to say. I wasn't even sure I agreed with him. How could church attendance be like circumcision?

"Let me ask you a question, Jake. How many ceiling tiles are there over your sanctuary?"

I didn't even have to think. "There are 312 complete ones and ninety-eight partials."

"And how do you know that?"

"I count them when I get bored."

"You must get bored a lot. Do you know how many others do, too? I met a guy once who even added up the hymn numbers on the tote board to see if they ever totaled 666. Don't you think people sharing God's life together wouldn't be so good at such things? Might it be a sign that something is wrong?"

Well, he might be right.

"What was your last thought as you arrived last Sunday morning?"

That required a bit more thought. "I was reviewing my notes, trying to think of an illustration I hadn't nailed down yet."

"Yes, but what did you say to yourself as you parked your car at the building?"

It took me a moment to fish it out of memory. "I'll be glad when this is over and I can get back home." I chuckled at the thought. "How did you know?"

"I didn't, but it doesn't surprise me. You know how many people think that way, even those paid to be there, like you? The routine eventually withers the life, no matter how good it is."

"So Davis's disillusionment is a good thing?" I asked incredulously.

"As is yours. When you realize that the routine you've stumbled into is not substantially contributing to your desire to know God better, some incredible things can happen. Sitting through the same program week after week wears thin. Aren't you tired of finding yourself, year after year, falling to the same temptations, praying the same unanswered prayers, and seeing no evidence that you are growing to discern God's voice with any greater clarity?"

"Yes, I am." Even I was surprised at how fast the answer came from my lips and the frustration that came with the words. "So why do we do it?"

"The answer to that, Jake, will tell you more about yourself than it will about the church. For now, let yourself be honest about your own boredom and disillusionment. This Father has never given up his desire to share the friendship with him that you had when you were thirteen."

"There have been other times since."

"Of course, but they did not endure long, did they? If they had you wouldn't have needed to cover up people like Davis and bolster his spirit with soothing but empty platitudes. People like him shouldn't be silenced as those who lack faith. Rather applaud them for their courage to treat their spiritual lives as something real. If the truth be told, Davis's honesty demonstrates more faith than your discomfort with it."

"What do I do, John? I want the life that you speak of."

"It won't take much from you, Jake. Just be real with Father and resist the urges to crawl back into your shell and silently endure lifelessness. Your struggle stems from the call of God's

Spirit to your own. Ask him to forgive you for substituting anything for the power of his love and invite him to show you how your diligent efforts at good works for him may be obscuring his love for you. Let God do the rest. He will draw you to himself."

I looked at my watch and knew I had to leave. "I'm sorry, I have to run. It's been a long time, John, but I'm going to give it a try!"

"Good. Won't it be a joy again to wake up confident about being loved by God every day, without having to earn it by any act of righteousness on your part? That is the secret to first love: don't try to earn it. Know that you are accepted and loved, not for what you can do for God, or somehow hoping that you will be worthy of his acceptance, but because his greatest desire is to have you as one of his children. Jesus came to remove any obstacle that would prevent that from happening."

I stood up to leave and grabbed John's hand. He squeezed mine and held it a moment. "This is not difficult, Jake. In this kingdom you really do get what you seek. That is the point of the whole thing. If you are looking for a relationship with God, you will find it."

"Then why don't I have it? I thought that's what I had been seeking all along."

"No doubt, it might have been at first. But this works the other way around as well. If you look at what you've ended up with, then you'll know what you've really been seeking!" He let go of my hand.

His words ended with such finality and I was so pressed to get back for my appointment that I simply nodded. I had no idea at the time what he meant.

"I hope I get to see you again."

"Oh, I think you will . . . in good time."

I thanked him, waved good-bye, and now late for my appointment, I took off running across the park. It has always amazed me that the greatest journeys of our lives begin so simply that we don't even know we've embarked on them until we're well down the road looking back. So it would be for me.

# 3

# This Is Christian Education?

My brief time in the park with John turned out to be more frustrating than helpful. Though I left that day excited about new possibilities and sailed through the rest of the day with none of the stress that had overwhelmed me earlier, the excitement quickly faded.

I had a hard time remembering all John had said and thought of a hundred questions I wished I had asked him. The fact that our time was so short and that he was unwilling to make any other arrangements made me angry. Who was he anyway? Could he be a madman stalking me?

But he didn't act mad. I had felt completely comfortable talking with him. It reminded me of the conversations I used to have with my dad before he passed away five years before in a car accident. Strangely, I felt a similar affection for John, whoever he was. He had fueled my hunger to know Jesus better, and it had not diminished in the months that passed, though my efforts to feed that hunger had failed miserably.

After that encounter I set aside forty-five minutes each morning before the rest of the family woke up to read the Bible and pray. Though I was faithful to do it every day, I couldn't tell any difference at all. The same stresses of work and home quickly crept back in. None of my prayers seemed to have any impact, even on those things I prayed about most diligently. I was discouraged but nonetheless remained persistent.

I had hoped by now I would have crossed paths with John again, but it hadn't happened. For a few weeks I caught myself looking for him everywhere. I didn't go to a store, eat at a restaurant, or even drive down the street without scanning every person to see if he was there. Occasionally I'd spot someone similar enough in build or gait to actually make my heart skip a beat. But as I got closer, my hopes were dashed time and time again. I even went out of my way a few times to check the bench at the park.

Imagine my surprise five months later when I saw his familiar face where I least expected to find it—peering through the diamond-shaped window of one of our sanctuary doors. It was Sunday morning during our largest worship service, and I was walking back up the center aisle with my best whatever-would-they-do-without-me face, having just eliminated an annoying hum from our state-of-the-art sound system. All I had done was jiggle a few wires plugged in beneath the stage, but that had done the trick.

I could feel people's eyes watching me walk up the aisle, even though the pastor was praying at the time. I kept my head down until I got near my row, when I took one quick look up the aisle. There he was. There was no mistaking those eyes, and my heart almost stopped as I recognized him.

Walking past my vacant seat, I slid out through the other half of the double doors. He stood there with a frown on his face, and I remember thinking how awkward and out of place he looked in our building. I don't know why it hit me that way. It wasn't his clothes. He was wearing a polo shirt and a pair of Dockers, more than appropriate for our informal California services.

We had others with similar beards and longer hair looking like holdovers from the hippie days. But he just somehow looked out of place.

"John, what are you doing here?" I whispered.

He turned toward me slowly, smiled to acknowledge my presence, and turned back to look inside. After a few moments he finally spoke: "I thought I'd see if you had some time to talk."

"Where have you been? I've looked for you everywhere."

He just kept staring through the window.

"I'd love to talk, but now is not a good time. Our biggest service is going on in there."

He didn't turn away from the window this time. "Yes, I noticed." I could hear the congregation standing up as the worship team began to play the introduction to the next song.

"How about later? After service?"

"I'm just passing through and thought I'd see how you were doing. Are you finding some answers to your questions?"

"I don't know. I'm doing everything I know to do. My devotional life is really coming around, more regular than it has ever been."

His silence told me I hadn't answered the question. I thought I might wait him out, but it got so awkward I couldn't help speaking again. "Oh . . . well . . . how can I say this? I guess not. In fact, it seems like the harder I try, the emptier and more frustrated I feel. It just doesn't seem worth the effort."

"Good." John nodded, still staring into the sanctuary. "Then you've learned something valuable, haven't you?"

"What?" I thought he'd misunderstood me. "I said it wasn't working. I've really been trying hard and nothing seems to be happening. How is that good? It only makes me angry."

"I understood," John replied, turning toward me again. "Do you want to know why? Come, I'll show you."

With that he turned and motioned with his head for me to follow and started toward the hallway that led to our education wing. As he walked away from me, I glanced back in the sanctuary. *I can't follow him now. I am supposed to be in that service. What if the sound system acts up again? What if . . . ?*

He was turning the corner. I'd lost him that way once

before, hadn't I? With no time to think it through, I dashed across the foyer to find him.

Rounding the corner I almost knocked over a young family coming toward us. I apologized for bumping into them, but they didn't seem to acknowledge it. Their faces melted with embarrassment.

"The one time we're late," the wife sighed, "and look who has to catch us—one of the pastors! Honest, we never come late." Over her shoulder I saw John had stopped to wait for me. He was leaning against the wall and watching our exchange. His eyebrows were arched upward and the smirk on his face looked like a playful *Caught you!*

Suddenly I felt like the church police. I had made a major announcement two Sundays before about how important it was to be on time so we didn't disrupt other worshipers by coming in late. I felt John's ears zeroing in on our conversation.

"We had a flat tire on the way," the husband offered.

"You're lucky. I'm not giving out tardy slips today." I laughed, hoping to smooth over their awkwardness and mine. "I'm just glad you're here." I hugged them both and walked with them to the sanctuary doors. As I pulled them open, an usher turned to help them find a seat.

I dashed across the lobby and turned up the hallway to the education wing. There he was, standing in front of our Sunday school bulletin board, his eyes arching over the top of it following the three-inch letters that read: *I was glad when they said to me, let us go to the house of the Lord.*

"What's that mean?" he asked, tracing the words with his index finger.

"That we should enjoy being in God's presence." My voice involuntarily turned up at the end, making my answer sound more like a question.

"Good answer. Why is it here?"

"That's our mission statement for Christian education," I answered, trying to appear nonchalant, but I knew he was driving at something. I just wasn't sure what it was.

"We are trying to provide an atmosphere where the kids really enjoy going to their classes."

"And 'the house of the Lord,' would that be this building?" He pointed down both ends of the hallway.

Oops. I didn't like where this was going. After a pause I responded, "Well, of course we all know it means something greater than this." I was desperate for a right answer, but I had the uneasy feeling that I didn't have one in my arsenal.

"But what do people think who read this?"

"They probably take it to mean coming to our church."

"Is that what you want them to think?"

I decided if I didn't answer we would move on. But he again let the silence hang longer than I could bear. "I guess we do."

"Don't you realize that the most powerful thing about the gospel is that it liberates us from the concept that God dwells in any building? For a people steeped in the rites of temple worship, this was either great or terrible news. His followers thought it was great. No longer did they have to think of God as cloaked in the recesses of the temple, available only to special people at select times."

I detected sadness in his voice and stood silent a moment.

"So then, Jake, if it isn't this building, where is God's house?"

"We are." I shook my head at how stupid that sign looked to me now. I wonder if John knew it had been my idea to begin with. I certainly was not going to tell him.

"Then how can anyone go to themselves?" He sighed with frustration. "Do you remember what Stephen said right before they picked up stones to kill him? 'The Most High does not dwell in houses made by human hands.' That's when they turned on him. It reminded them of Jesus' challenge to destroy the temple and rebuild it in three days. People can get very touchy about their buildings, especially if they think God dwells in them."

I didn't say anything. I just nodded in agreement.

"And are they glad when they come?"

It took me a moment to figure out what he meant. "We hope so. We go to an awful lot of work."

"It certainly looks that way." John's eyes were roving all over the bulletin board, where announcements about training seminars, staff meetings, class activities, and request forms for supplies spilled over the edges.

"A quality program takes a lot of work."

"Undoubtedly. And not a little bit of guilt, either, to say nothing of manipulation." I followed his eyes to the center of our teacher-recruitment poster. It was a full-color depiction of a teenager in punk garb on an urban street at night. In big letters down the left side it read: *If only someone would have taken the time to teach him about Jesus. Volunteer today.*

"Guilt? Manipulation? We're not trying to make anyone feel guilty, just giving them facts."

He shook his head and started walking down the hall. I glanced back toward the sanctuary, knowing that's where I should have been. But instead I quickly decided I'd better stay with John, who had already turned down another hallway.

As I rounded the corner I could hear the strains of children singing,

> *Good morning to you! Good morning to you!*
> *We're all in our places, with bright shining faces.*

John was peeking through the partially opened door. Rows of first graders sat facing the teacher in their miniature chairs. As the song ended, there was lots of squirming, poking, and laughter. One boy dressed in a bright blue sweater vest turned around to stick out his tongue at one of the girls. When he did he caught sight of us looking at him and immediately turned back around and pretended to pay attention.

We couldn't see the teacher from our vantage point, but we could hear her pleading voice shouting from our right.

"Let's say our memory verse!" she shouted. "Come on! Settle down or there will be no snack later." Apparently the threat was effective because the room went silent.

"Who knows their memory verse?"

Hands shot up throughout the classroom.

"Let's say it together. 'I was glad when they said to me...'" The staccato voices never changed pitch. "Let us go to the house of the Lord, Psalm 122 verse one" (NLT). Most voices had faded out for the reference except for one girl. She clearly wanted everyone to know she knew it.

"And what does it mean?" the teacher shouted above the rising noise.

Two hands shot up, one of them from the same girl who had repeated the reference so loudly.

"Sherri, tell us!"

"That's my girl," I whispered to John.

The girl stood up. "It means that we should enjoy coming to church, because this is where God lives."

"That's right," the teacher said as I felt my face flush with embarrassment.

I shrugged my shoulders when John turned to smile playfully at me. Then he soundlessly mouthed two words: "It's working." The smile on his face pulled the plug on my embarrassment. He had made it clear that he wasn't there to shame me.

When we both turned back to the class, the teacher was passing out golden stars made from foil for children to stick up on a chart on the wall. We used them for things like attendance, memory verses, and the children bringing their Bibles. The class was in chaos as kids were getting their stars, dodging one another while finding their names on the chart, licking their stickers, and putting them in place.

When the class got back to their seats, the teacher went to the chart and pointed down a few of the rows. "Look at all the stars Bobby has. Sherri is doing well, too, as are Liz and Kelly. Don't forget the five top Superstars will get a special prize at the end of the quarter. So let's work hard. Make sure you come every week, bring your Bible, and work on your memory verse."

"Making a list and checking it twice?" John sang softly. It took me a minute to realize that was a Santa Claus song, not one of ours. "Seen enough?" he asked, turning toward me.

"What? Oh, I'm just watching you. I already know what goes on in there."

"I'm not sure you do." John turned away from the window and walked a little farther down the hall, stopping finally alongside the water fountain. His right arm crossed his chest with his left elbow resting on it, his left hand massaging his down-turned forehead.

"Jake, did you see that boy sitting next to your daughter in the shorts and light yellow T-shirt?"

"No, not specifically."

"Well, I'm not surprised. There wasn't much to look at really. He wasn't making any noise, just sitting there with his head down and his arms folded."

"Oh, I know who you're talking about. That must be Benji."

"Benji. Did you notice that he didn't know one word of the memory verse and he didn't even go up to get the star he earned just for coming today?"

"No, I didn't."

"How do you think all that made him feel?"

"I hope it made him want to do better—to bring his Bible, to come more often and to memorize his verses. That's how we motivate the kids. Everyone does it. It is for a good purpose."

"But how is he ever going to compete against . . . Sherri, was it? Are his parents as supportive as you are?"

"He only has his mom and has never seen his dad. She's a hard worker and loves him a lot, but you know how tough single parenting can be. I can't even imagine it myself."

"Do you think Benji will go away encouraged?"

"That's what we're hoping." I thought of Benji sitting there with a distant look I'd seen so many times. "But I guess we'd have to say it hasn't worked for him yet, although it works for most of the other kids. We have one of the most successful children's ministries in the city."

"Is it your point that Sherri's feelings of accomplishment are worth Benji's shame?"

I wanted to answer his question, but couldn't think of anything to say that didn't sound incredibly stupid.

"Did you go to Sunday school, Jake, when you were young?"

"I did. My parents raised us at church. I once memorized 153 Bible verses in one three-month contest."

John's eyes popped open. "Really? And what drove you to that?"

"The winner got a brand-new Bible."

"And I suppose you probably didn't even need one."

I paused a moment, remembering that my parents had

bought me a Bible shortly before that. I cocked my head and squinted at him bewilderedly. How did he know?

"The ones who usually win don't need the prize."

"I did have another Bible, but this one was special. I won it."

"A hundred and fifty three? That's a lot of verses."

"Memorizing has always come easy for me. I just read a verse over a couple of times and I've got it. It really wasn't hard. Most verses I memorized in the morning before church."

"How many verses did the second-place person memorize?"

"About thirty-five if I remember right. I really blew them away."

"And you're thinking all of this is a healthy demonstration of spiritual fervor?"

*Well, now that you question it, maybe not,* I thought, but remained silent.

"What else did you win?"

"When I was around ten, I received a gold-plated pin for two years of consecutive Sunday school attendance. The pastor gave it to me one Sunday morning in front of the whole church. You should have heard the applause. I will never forget how special I felt."

"It gave you something to live for, didn't it?"

"What do you mean?"

"Isn't that what you've been seeking ever since, that feeling of being special?"

It was as if a veil had just been lifted off my eyes. Most of my decisions had been made when I was craving the recognition and honor of other people. I loved people's approval and often fantasized about it. If the truth be told, that was probably the strongest draw in leaving my real estate job and taking a position in ministry, where I could be up front, well known, and appreciated. "Did that one moment cause me to seek approval constantly?"

"Of course not. It was a lot of moments like that, exposing and nourishing a desire you already had way down here." He pointed to my chest. "Who doesn't want to be liked and appreciated? It's an easy thing to use when you're trying to motivate people to do good things. The larger question is, did all that memorization and attendance help you know Father better?

"What's easier for you to do, pursue a relationship with

the Father or your own sense of personal success? That's the real test. It seems to me you wouldn't be so desperate if the pursuit had really taught you how to know Father's love. Instead, you're so busy seeking everyone's approval, you don't realize you already have his."

"What do you mean? How could I have his approval when I'm still struggling so?"

"Because you are struggling for the wrong thing. You think that you can earn Father's approval. We're approved not because of anything we can do, but because of what he did for us on the cross. Honestly, Jake, there's not one thing you can do to make him love you any more today, and there's not one thing you can do to make him love you any less, either. He just loves you.

"It is your security in that love that will change you, not your struggle to try and earn it."

My eyes began to moisten with tears. He had unlocked something I'd never considered before.

"So all my efforts are in vain?"

"If they are directed at trying to get him to love you more, yes, they are. If you never counseled another person or taught another class, Jake, he would love you no less."

*What?* I was speechless. I wanted to believe him, but he had just challenged everything I had ever worked for. While it would explain why so many of my efforts had fallen short, I had no idea how to embrace what he'd just said. Was I really trying to earn what he had already given?

After a few moments, John pushed away from the wall and started walking farther down the hallway and I took up my position alongside him.

"You know that morning you got the attendance pin? If that pastor had really loved you, do you know what he would have said? 'Ladies and gentlemen, we want to introduce a young man who has just completed a two-year span of never missing a Sunday school class. We want to pray for him because that means his family's priorities are so askew that for the last two years they never took a vacation together. It means he probably came here when he was sick and should have been home resting.

It means that winning this gold-plated trinket and your approval is more important to him than being your brother. And not one day of his attendance will draw him any closer to God.'"

"That might have been a little rude," I countered.

"And a setup, certainly, Jake. But if he had, perhaps you wouldn't pursue the approval that does far more to distract you from God than it does to open you up to him."

"What you're saying, then, is that using approval to reward Sherri is not only hurtful to Benji, but harmful to Sherri, too?"

He punched the air with his index finger as if to tap an imaginary button. "Bingo! Do you know that more than 90 percent of children who grow up in Sunday school leave the congregation when they leave their parents' home?"

"I have heard that. We blame that on the public schools that disaffect children from their faith."

John raised his eyebrows incredulously. "Really? That's convenient."

"Well, we're doing *our* part," I said defensively.

"In more ways than you've seen so far."

"So you're saying everything bad I learned about God I learned in Sunday school." I could hear the mockery and frustration in my own voice.

"Well, not quite. I didn't say it was all bad."

"How could it be? We teach the kids about God and the Bible, and how to be good Christians." My voice faded out as it dawned on me that learning about God and what it means to be a good Christian was not the same as learning to walk with him.

"What I want you to see is that laced through the wonderful things you have here is a system of religious obligation that distorts it all. Until you see that, you'll never know what it means to walk with Father."

"Why's that?"

"He's done too much to free you from it, to reward it. Certainly everything else in your life might be based on performance, but not your relationship with him. It's not based on what we do, but on what he's done."

"So I've been trying too hard, is that what you're saying?

Is that why my efforts aren't working? Don't we have to do our part?" I looked back at John.

"Not exactly," said John with a slight chuckle under his breath. "But you are getting close. It's that you're trying to earn a relationship you'll never earn. Men and women might give you acclaim for memorizing Scriptures or attending services, but those are never going to be enough to earn a relationship. Besides, you're pursuing them not because you want to know God, but because you want people to think that you're spiritual. And you know what? That is what you're getting out of it."

"So that's what Jesus meant when he said the Pharisees were doing things to be seen by others and they were getting their reward. But that's not what I really want."

"Good. Can't you see that the trail you're on doesn't go where you've been told it goes? It will make you a good Christian in the eyes of others, but it will not let you know him." John didn't seem to be walking anyplace in particular. Aimlessly we strolled past classrooms and occasionally a person rushing through the hallways. I was so engaged in our discussion that I hadn't noticed people giving us strange looks. I would pay for that later.

"So I can become an incredible Christian as far as everyone around me is concerned, yet miss the real heart of it?"

"Isn't that where you are? Look at this massive program here. Look at these buildings, the needs of the children, and the demands of the machinery. What does it need to exist?"

"Obviously it needs people and money and an aura of spirituality, I guess."

"And that's what it rewards, doesn't it? How do you remain a member in good standing here?"

"Consistent attendance, giving, and not living in obvious sin."

"All sins?"

"What do you mean?"

"Well, I don't know about this place, but in others there are some sins that aren't allowed at all—usually sexual sins or teaching something the leaders don't like. But others just as destructive are ignored, such as gossip, arrogance, or condemning others. Sometimes these are even rewarded, because we can use those to get people to act the way we want them to."

Even our sense of sin was selective. I could see it now. I knew people who were able to exploit the system for their own gain, even if it hurt others. I'd done it myself.

"Isn't it interesting how a group of people who get together regularly will eventually develop an *esprit de corps*, even down to how people dress and talk, what reactions they allow, and what songs they like to sing? Isn't it pretty clear here what being a good Christian is, and isn't a big part of that not to make any waves or ask questions that make people uncomfortable?"

He got that right.

"One of the most significant lessons Jesus taught his disciples was to stop looking for God's life in the regimen of rituals and rules. He came not to refurbish their religion, but to offer them a relationship. Was it just a coincidence that he found more sick people on the Sabbath? Of course not! He wanted his disciples to know that the rules and traditions of men get in the way of the power and life of his Father.

"And it can be pretty captivating, too, because we all do what we do thinking it pleases God. No prison is as strong as religious obligation. It takes us captive even while we're patting ourselves on the back. I walked past a synagogue yesterday and the rabbi came outside and asked if I could come in and turn some lights on for him. Someone had forgotten to do it the day before, and he couldn't do it himself without breaking the Sabbath."

"That's pretty silly, isn't it?"

"To you it might be, and so would some of your rules and rituals seem to him."

"Some of mine? I don't do anything like that about the Sabbath."

"Of course not, but what if you missed Sunday morning services for a month—just stayed home or gave your tithe to the poor instead of putting it in the offering plate?"

"Those are the same thing?"

John nodded.

"Yes, but I do those things not because I think they're law, but because I am free to."

"The rabbi would say no different. But if you were honest,

you'd see that you do them because you believe they make you more acceptable to God and make him more favorably disposed to you. If you didn't do them, you'd feel guilty."

At the time I didn't understand all the implications of his words, but I knew he was right. When our church stopped having Sunday night services a few years back, it really bothered me. I had been to church virtually every Sunday night of my life and it took me two years before I could sit home without feeling guilty or scheduling some kind of fellowship time with people in the church so I'd feel productive.

"That's why you can never relax, Jake. Even on your day off, I bet you have a hard time just doing nothing. You feel guilty if you think you're wasting time."

As his words were soaking in, another song drifted up the hallway from one of the classes: "Oh be careful, little eyes, what you see…" The last line warned that God would be watching over their every action. Though it said he'd do so "in love," I don't think any child singing that song ever believed it. To a child, this was God behind the bushes with his radar gun, ready to catch them lest they make a mistake.

"There's the worst of it," John said, shaking his head in obvious pain. "I hate hearing little kids sing that song."

For a moment I couldn't figure out what he was talking about. The song was familiar. I had sung it since I was a child and had taught it to my own children because they enjoyed acting it out. Besides, I hoped knowing that God would see everything would help them make right choices. "Are you saying there's something wrong with that song?"

"You tell me."

"I don't know. It talks about the Father's love for us and his desire to keep us from doing evil."

"But what does he become in that song?"

"I don't know what you're driving at."

"It takes wonderful words like 'Father' and 'love' and turns God into the divine policeman, waiting behind the billboard with his radar gun. Who wants to grow close to a Father like that? We can't love what we fear. You can't foster a relationship with someone who is always checking your performance to make sure it's adequate enough to merit his friendship. The more you focus on your own needs and failures, the more distant Father will seem to you. Guilt does that. It shoves us away from God in our time of need, instead of allowing us to run to him, presenting our greatest failures and questions so that we might receive his mercy and grace. Now we've invoked God and his punishment to shore up our sense of what it means to be a good Christian.

"Do you see a Father here who understands our bent toward sin, who knows how weak we are, whose love wants to meet us in our sinfulness and transform us to be his children, not based on our efforts but his?"

"I don't think I've ever thought about that."

"Oh, yes, you have. Every time you sang it you thought of things your eyes had seen and your ears had heard that God would disapprove of. It made you feel bad, but feeling bad didn't make you do any better. So intellectually you are still thinking of Father's love, but intuitively you are being distanced from him. That's the worst thing that religion does. Who is going to draw near to God if he's always trying to catch people at their worst moments, or always punishing them for their failures? We're too weak for a God like that. We use guilt to conform people's behavior, never realizing the same guilt will keep them far from God."

We had come back to the foyer again. John stopped walking and leaned back against the wall. I stood there with him for a moment. "No wonder we're always checking up on people, encouraging them to do the right thing, and rarely do we spend time helping them understand what it is to relate to a Father who knows everything about them and yet loves them completely."

He nodded. "That's why Jesus' death is so threatening to those bred in religious obligation. If you were sick of it and realized that it alone couldn't open the doors to the relationship your heart cried out for, the cross was the greatest news of all. If, however, you made your living or earned your status in the system, the cross was a scandal. Now we can be loved without doing one thing to earn it."

"But won't people misuse that as an excuse to serve themselves?"

"Of course, but just because people abuse something doesn't make it wrong. If they want to live for themselves, it doesn't matter that they claim some kind of false grace. But to people who really want to know God, he's the only one who can open the door."

"That's why my last few months have been so fruitless?"

"Exactly. Relationship with him is his gift, freely given. The point of the cross was that he could do for us what we could never do ourselves. The key is not found in how much you love him, but in how much he loves you. It begins in him. Learn that and your relationship will begin to grow."

"Then most of what we're doing here is incredibly misdirected. What would happen if we stopped it all?"

The closing song filled the foyer as the ushers threw the doors open, ready for the congregation to exit. Had I been gone that long?

"That really isn't the issue, is it, Jake? I'm talking about your relationship with the living God, not fixing this institution. Sure, it would make for a drastic change. Instead of putting on a show, we would gather to celebrate his work in the lives of his people. Instead of figuring out how we can get people to act more 'Christian,' we would help people get to know Jesus better and let him change them from the inside out. It would revolutionize the life of the church and the lives of its people. But it doesn't begin there," he said, motioning toward the sanctuary doors, "but here," and he tapped himself on the chest.

One of the ushers looked over and saw me. "Jake, there you are. Pastor was asking for you during the service. The sound system kept acting up and he kept calling for you."

"Oh, crud!" I moaned. "I've got to go," I said to John as I dashed through the doors just a step ahead of the flowing river of humanity.

I didn't know what happened to John after that, but I knew there had to be some changes in my own life, and to that Sunday school bulletin board.

# 4

# Why Your Promises Haven't Worked

I hate getting up at six in the morning for a breakfast meeting and having everyone else fail to show up.

This is an accountability group, after all.

Five of us formed it after a men's retreat six months earlier, promising to hold ourselves accountable to being good husbands, involved fathers, and committed believers. Attendance after the first few weeks had been sporadic, but that day only one other guy showed and he hadn't been to a meeting in at least two months. In fact, we'd given up on him.

Bob Miller, one of our council members, came only to tell me afterward that he and Joyce were separated. I was hoping Gil Rodriguez would show up because he was the only one I could talk to about my escalating problems at church, for which I mostly blamed John. So instead of unburdening myself, I spent the whole time talking about Bob's separation.

He'd been married to Joyce for more than thirty years and raised three children, and until that moment I'd thought they were one of our model couples. Since Bob was one of our council members, I knew this was going to reflect poorly on our congregation.

Joyce had accidentally stumbled across some pornography on his computer and had been so humiliated she demanded that he leave. I was sure it was a mistake, but Bob assured me it was not. It was a battle from his younger years that he had seemingly put behind him. "The Internet just made it too easy," he confessed. He didn't have to risk renting a video or purchasing a magazine in public.

During our conversation I kept hearing laughter across the partition in another section of the restaurant. I remembered thinking how out of place the laughter seemed with the grief going on right in front of me. How dare anyone have that much fun this time of the morning around people in so much pain!

I tried everything I could think of to help Bob fix it, but he said it was impossible. The latest incident was not the whole problem. Their marriage had been steadily dying since the kids left home and this was only the last straw in a long string of painful incidents. We finally ran out of time as Bob had to leave for work.

We got up and walked to the cash register to pay our checks. I was seething with anger at the other guys for not showing up and at Bob for being such an idiot. As I got change back from the waitress at the cash register, I looked up to see a familiar face. It had been nearly two months since our tour through the Sunday school wing. Our eyes met and he seemed as genuinely surprised as I was.

"John? What are you doing here?"

A big smile broke out across his face and he answered with a chuckle in his voice, "Jake, how are you doing?" He came over and shook my hand.

I tried to introduce him to Bob but didn't know John's last

name. "Bob, this is John, a friend I met a few months ago." Turning to John, I added, "I'm sorry, I don't know if I've ever heard your last name."

"John is good enough," he said, shaking Bob's hand.

Bob smiled back, but it quickly gave way to a strained look on his face. "Are you the . . . ?" Then, turning to me, he started again, "Is this the guy . . . ?" He stopped again, fumbling awkwardly.

I was afraid of what he'd say next and gave him my best, please-be-careful face. "Is this the guy who got you into all that trouble?"

I looked at John sheepishly as he turned toward me. "I wouldn't put it that way."

"Maybe it was someone else." Bob glanced at his watch, announced that he was late for work already, and with a wave was quickly out the door.

"I'm surprised to see you." I turned back to John.

"I had breakfast with an old friend this morning. He had to leave and I've still got almost an hour before my bus departs." He nodded in the direction of the bus depot down the street.

"Where are you headed?"

"I have a meeting upstate this evening."

"Were you going to look me up?"

"I obviously didn't need to, Jake. I really didn't have much time to arrange anything, but if you want to join me at my table, I've got some time now."

I followed him across the room and sat down at the table in the corner where all the laughter had come from earlier. "Was that you laughing so hard over here, or was that another table?" I asked, sizing up the room.

"Oh, that was Phillip! I wish I'd known you were here because I want you two to meet—perhaps in a future trip. He's on a similar journey to yours, and he's just surfaced from some painful and deep waters. He's just like a kid splashing around the summer pond. His joy is even more infectious than his laugh."

"I'm glad someone is having fun," I said, the sarcasm dripping from my lips.

"That doesn't sound good."

"It's been horrible since I last saw you and this morning really topped it off. No one showed up for our accountability group, except Bob who hasn't met us for a long time. He only came to tell me he and his wife are separated because she found some pornography on his computer. He's a leader at the church, too. What a mess!"

"You seem really angry."

"This is going to hurt the church."

"Is that why you're angry at him?"

That was the first time that morning I stopped to think how I felt about Bob. I had been so upset with his separation and how it would affect the church, I really hadn't thought about Bob.

"I didn't think I was mad at Bob. I was mad at his failure and . . ."

"And what it is going to cost you."

"I don't know if I thought of it that way, but now that you mention it I was pretty hard on him. I guess I blame him for not being more consistent with the group and admitting his struggle."

"Accountability is not for those who struggle, Jake. It's for those who succeed."

"But aren't we accountable to one another?"

"Where did you get that idea?"

"It's in the Bible, isn't it?"

"Can you show me where?" John reached down and pulled a Bible off the booth seat next to him and tossed it on the table.

I picked it up and started to thumb through it while my mind raced to find a passage. I couldn't come up with one. I even glanced through the concordance but recognized all those passages referred to our giving account to God, not to one another. "Doesn't Hebrews talk about people being accountable to leadership in some way?"

"No," John said as he chuckled, "it talks about leaders giving an account for the lives they touch. All the accountability in Scripture is linked to God, not to other brothers and sisters. When we hold one another accountable, we are really usurping God's place. It's why we end up hurting one another so deeply."

"How are we going to change, then? We've taught people that they grow in Christ by making a commitment to doing what's right and then following through. We need to help one another do that!"

"How well is that working for you, Jake, or for the rest of the group?"

"Not very well, I'd have to admit. But that's because people aren't committed enough."

"You really think so?"

I'd heard that tone of voice before and knew that at least John didn't see it that way. I hesitated to answer.

"Do you know what all this commitment talk produces?" John asked.

"It helps people try to live better, doesn't it?"

"It looks like that." John shook his head and let out a deep sigh. "But it doesn't work. We're not changed by the promises we make to God, but by the promises he makes to us. When we make commitments that we can live up to only for a brief period, our guilt multiplies when we fail. Upset that God doesn't do more to help us, we usually end up medicating our guilt with something like drugs, alcohol, food, shopping, or anything else that dulls the pain, or it creeps out of us through anger or lust."

"Are you saying that's what happened to Bob?"

"I don't know Bob, but I'd say it's likely. Did he feel safe enough to come and share his deepest temptation?"

"Obviously not!" I shook my head in frustration. "A lot of our wives say we need a men's retreat every month to keep us motivated enough. I sometimes think they're right."

"Yes, it's easy to come back on a high and keep your commitments for a few weeks, but what happens when the glory of that fades and it's no fun treating your wife like a queen or spending time with your children when there are more pressing demands at work? You finally give in because nothing has changed on the inside. This is an outward-in approach, based on human effort, and it just won't work."

"So you're saying that our approach is only producing more sin?"

"For most people, yes, I am. That's why Bob doesn't want to come and no one else does, either. Even when they are there, they probably aren't telling the real stories of their struggles. They would feel too bad about themselves. Instead, they confess to acceptable sins like busyness, anger, or gossip.

"That's the worst part of religious thinking. It takes our best ambitions and uses them against us. People who are trying to be more godly actually become more captive to their appetites and desires. That's exactly what happened to Eve. She just wanted to be like God, which is also exactly what God wants for us. It wasn't what she wanted that got her in trouble, but that she relied on her own strength to get her there.

"Paul recognized there are three roads in this life, when most of us only recognize two. We tend to think of our lives as a choice between doing bad and doing good. Paul saw two different ways we could try to do good—one makes us work hard to submit to God's rules. That one fails every time. Even when he described himself as following all of God's rules externally, he also called himself the worst sinner alive because of the hate and anger in his heart. Sure, he could conform his outward behavior to fit the rules, but it only pushed his problems deeper. He was, you remember, out killing God's people in God's name."

"Yes, but Paul is talking about the Old Testament law there. We're not following the law. We're seeking to live by New Testament principles."

"No, he's not, Jake. Paul is talking about religion—man's effort to appease God by his own work. If we do what he wants, he will be good to us, and if we don't, then bad things will happen in our lives. On its best day, this approach will allow us to be smugly self-righteous, which is a trap all its own. On its worst days it will heap guilt upon us greater than we can bear. Your 'New Testament principles' are just another way of living to the law. You're still caught up in the process of trying to get God to reward you for doing good."

"So trying to do good can be a bad thing?" I couldn't believe what I was hearing.

"If you go about it that way, yes. But Paul saw another way to live in God's life that was so engaging, it transformed his entire life. He knew that our failures all result from the fact that we just don't trust God to take care of us. As Paul grew to know God better, he discovered that he could trust God's love for him. The more he grew to trust God's love, the freer he was from those desires that consumed him. Only by trusting Jesus can anyone experience real freedom."

"Won't people just use that for an excuse to do whatever feels good and ignore what God wants?"

"Sure, some will. Many already have. But those who really know who God is will want to be like him."

"We have to have a standard, though, so people can know what that is."

That's when he dropped the bombshell that exploded every remaining preconception I had of the Christian life: "Jake, when are you going to get past the mistaken notion that Christianity is about ethics?"

*What?* I looked up at him and could not get one coherent thought from my brain to my mouth. *If it isn't about ethics, what is it about?* I had been raised all of my life to believe that Christianity was an ethic for life that would earn me a place in God's heart. I didn't even know where to put this last statement, but he seemed content just to let it hang there.

Finally I found something to say. "I don't even know how to respond to that. I've lived my whole life in Christ thinking this was all about ethics."

"And that is why you're missing it. You're so caught up in a system of reward and punishment that you're missing the simple relationship he wants to have with you."

"How else are we going to know how God feels about us if we don't live up to his standards?"

"That's where you have it backward, Jake. We don't get his love by living up to his standards. We find his love in the most broken places of our lives. As we let him love us there and discover how to love him in return, we'll find our lives changing in that relationship."

"How can that be? Don't we have to walk away from sin to know him?"

"Walking toward him *is* walking away from sin. The better you know him, the freer from it you will be. But you can't walk away from sin, Jake. Not in your own strength! Everything he wants to do in you will get done as you learn to live in his love. Every act of sin results from your mistrust of his love and intentions for you. We sin to fill up broken places, to try to fight for what we think is best for us, or to react to our guilt and shame. Once you discover how much he loves you, all that changes. As you grow in trusting him, you will find yourself increasingly free from sin."

"It sounds so easy when you say it, John. But learning to live that way would be the opposite of everything I've been taught."

"That's why it's called 'good news,' Jake."

I knew sorting this conversation out would take some time, and I hadn't even sorted out the last one yet. Which reminded me, I was mad at John. I wasn't sure how to bring it up, but as I saw John start to gather his things together, I thought I'd better get it in quick.

"Will this get me in as much trouble as our last conversation?" My tone had turned a bit menacing.

"Is this what Bob was talking about earlier? What happened, Jake?"

"Your little visit caused quite an uproar. Pastor Jim was angry because the short in the sound system kept popping up during his sermon. It distracted him and he thought it ruined his message. I should have been there to help fix it and instead I was giving a tour of our education wing to someone whose last name I don't even know. That didn't go over too well. I couldn't even tell him where you lived. He was livid, accusing me of giving some potential pedophile a tour of our children's wing."

"That's quite a leap," John answered calmly. I thought the accusation would anger him, but it didn't even faze him.

"I assured him it wasn't true, but he asked me how he could trust someone who wasn't committed enough to be where he was supposed to be that morning. He exploded at me, John. I've never seen him like that. We've been close friends for more than two decades and continued that friendship even after I came on staff. He's loved me through my worst moments and supported me when others tried to tear me down. Now he picks at everything I do and we don't spend any relaxed time together."

"All of that changed after my last visit? Didn't you tell me in the park a few months back that things were already tense between you?"

I paused to think about it. "Now that you mention it, it has been going on for quite a while. He's been difficult to work with for probably six months or more. He's been distant and hardly ever responds to my suggestions."

"It sounds like something else is going on there."

"Whatever it is, this just made it worse. He didn't even like any of the changes I made."

"Changes? What changes?"

"The ones you told me to make."

"I didn't tell you to make any changes, did I, Jake?"

"I got rid of that sign you didn't like, about our church being the house of God, and that guilt-inducing poster."

John chuckled playfully and shook his head as if I'd just made an innocent gaffe. "I bet that went over well."

"It's not funny, John. A few days after I changed the bulletin board, Jill Harper, the lady who cut out all those letters and made the poster at my request, came by my office. She asked what happened to the bulletin board. I told her I was uncomfortable with some of the messages it gave out and wanted to redo it. She was furious that I had changed it without consulting her. I apologized, but it didn't do much good. She doesn't want to talk about it anymore and I think she's been spreading her anger to others on the children's ministry team. Many of them are upset with me, too."

"What about?"

"A few weeks ago I presented a new proposal to shift the priority of our children's program to fit what we talked about when you were here."

"Uh-oh!"

"Uh-oh? I was so excited. I spent a lot of time and printed up a ten-page paper on how we could refocus our classes and retrain our teachers. I was just certain they would be as thrilled as I to put this ministry on a better footing. I listed specific recommendations about giving up our star charts and changing our songs to be more grace-centered."

"And?"

"They thought I was accusing them of being Pharisees. They said they believed in grace as much as anyone else and told me they had all grown up with those charts, and that putting up stars gives children a feeling of accomplishment. I didn't know what to say, I was so surprised. In the heat of the battle, I couldn't even remember what you'd said. The night was a disaster."

"I can imagine, Jake. I'm sorry it was so hurtful."

"I don't even know what I did wrong, John. Life at the church was tough before. Now it's a nightmare and I don't think the pastor has any respect for me anymore. My stomach is always in knots."

"Jake, if you listen to nothing else I say, listen to this: don't use our conversations to try to change others. I'm only trying to help you learn to live in God's freedom. Until they are looking for the same things you are, people will not understand and you'll be accused of far worse. You're trying to live what I said without letting God make it real in you. It won't work that way. You'll just end up hurting a lot of people and hurting yourself in the process."

John slid off the chair and stood up, fishing some bills out of his pocket to leave a tip.

"That's for sure," I said, getting up with him.

John told me he had to get to the depot to catch his bus. I offered to drive him over to help save him some time and also to give me some time to finish the conversation. We kept talking as we walked toward the register, paid his check, and walked to my car.

"You're not finding his presence to be any more real for you than when we first talked, are you?"

"Why would you say that?"

"Because you're still trying to make others do it, instead of living it yourself. It's natural for us to deal with our own emptiness by trying to get others around us to change. That's why so much body life today is built around accountability and human effort: if we could just get everyone else to do what's right, everything would be better for us."

"Wouldn't it?"

"No, Jake! We're not ever going to get it all right. People are going to mess up. Sorting out a relationship with Jesus is a lifetime journey. The life of faith is struggle enough in a broken world without us complicating it for other believers. Why do you think you weren't there for Bob and now your pastor isn't there for you?"

"I don't know."

"Because real body life isn't built on accountability. It's built on love. We're to encourage one another in the journey without conforming people to the standard we think they need."

"That sounds like relativism, John!"

"It's not, it simply respects the process God uses to bring people into truth. I'm not talking about different things being true for different people, but about people discovering that truth in different time frames. If we hold people accountable, they will never learn to live in love. We'll reward those who are better at putting on a front and miss those who are in the real struggle of learning to live in Jesus."

"I can't even imagine sharing that kind of journey with others."

"It's the best, Jake! It opens the door for people to be authentic and known exactly for who they are. It encourages them to draw near to Jesus, not try to fix everybody with our answers for the universe."

"Where can I find that, John? Is there a place like that in Kingston?"

"Jake, you misunderstand. It is not a place, it's a way of living alongside other believers. Are there others who want to live this way? Sure. And you'll find one another in time. But first, let it change you."

I pulled up to the bus depot and stopped and John

popped the handle on the door. "I'd better run, Jake, I'm going to be late for the bus."

"Can't you give me a number where I can get ahold of you in case I need to talk?"

"That's not as easy to do as you might think," John said, stepping out of the car, closing the door. "I'll find you again, I'm sure of that," he said, leaning in through the open window.

"I'm not."

"Take care, Jake. You're on the right path. It may get worse before it gets better, but it's the same with surgery. When it does finally get better, it's going to really get better!"

"It doesn't feel that way."

"I know. Getting to the end of ourselves is not the fun part. It's just the first part. At that time, the closer we get, the farther we feel we are from him. That's why I want to encourage you to just keep hanging in there with Jesus. He'll sort all of this out in ways you'd never believe if I could tell you today."

"Thanks, John. That helps." As he turned to walk away, I suddenly remembered one thing I hadn't asked him. "Can't you at least tell me your last name?"

The taxi honking behind me must have drowned out my request because John walked through the doors without turning back.

# 5

# Love with a Hook

I'd gone up there to get away from it all, but I ended up bringing it all with me. I don't think a single minute of my waking hours had been free of thoughts about what was going on back home. My emotions seethed with frustration and anger that even this pristine setting could not soothe.

Nellie Lake is one of my favorite spots on earth. It lies in the high Sierras at the end of a five-mile trail that snakes almost straight uphill. They say in California if you hike twenty minutes from the road you lose 90 percent of the fishermen. It is a two-and-a-half-hour hike and I have rarely seen anyone else here even in the middle of summer. This was early September and I had the whole lake to myself on that crisp afternoon.

It's a small lake, but I'd always caught plenty of good-size rainbow trout there. What's more, it's the only place where I've caught fish that actually act like the fish on the covers of those outdoor magazines. When you hook them, they leap straight out of the water in a desperate attempt to throw your hook and swim free. Of course, I'm certain I love that action far more than the fish do.

Laurie had gone out of town to visit her parents for a week. On a whim, and in a fit of frustration, I decided to pull our tent trailer up to Huntington Lake for a few days of personal retreat. I had already typed up my resignation but hid it in my desk until I could think things through.

I had taken to heart my last conversations with John and in the six months since I'd seen him, my relationship with God had really begun to grow. I was more aware of his presence throughout the day. I was just beginning to learn how to trust him more than my own efforts, when the church at home erupted in conflict. Somehow I had lost sight of God in it all and found myself once again looking for John's familiar face in every crowd of people I passed. I had finally given up and decided to run away, if only for a few days.

For the last two hours I had perched myself on the south side of Nellie Lake and had fished with a vengeance. Even though I had caught almost twenty fish and enjoyed reeling them to shore, such moments provided only a momentary distraction to the greater pain that seethed in my gut. As soon as I would release them and rebait my hook, I was right back fuming inside. I had seen some horrible conflicts during my years in real estate, but I'd never seen a group of people treat one another with such hostility and deceit while working so hard to appear sweet and innocent.

"Idiots!" I exclaimed across the lake, exhaling some anger while my fishing line sat idle in the lake.

"I hope you're not talking about me." The familiar voice spilled off the hill behind me. Startled, I jumped and whipped around. John, with a backpack over his shoulders, was making his way down the hillside to the lakeshore.

I almost tripped over my pole when I tried to lay it down

and turn to greet him in one motion. "What are you doing up here?"

"I come up here every year about this time for two weeks or so just to hike in the high country and enjoy some peace and quiet. I don't often find people here, especially those I know."

"Neither do I. That's what I like about it," I said.

"You want me to go?"

"Are you kidding?" He was the one person whose presence I could welcome up there right then.

He unclasped his backpack and slid it off his shoulders, placing it against an old tree stump. Stretching his back, he asked, "Do you come up here often?"

"Not really. Once a year at most." Suddenly my fishing pole started to quiver and fell off the log where I had propped it. I grabbed it and started to reel in the line. What looked like an eighteen-inch rainbow broke through the water, leaping toward me. My line suddenly went limp as the hook popped out of his mouth. John and I chuckled as I brought the line into shore and put the pole down. Fishing was now the furthest thing from my mind.

"Another one goes free," John said. Then he sat down on the log and asked, "So who are the idiots? The fish?"

My face flushed as I recalled my outburst of a few seconds before. "No, the fishing has been incredible. It's the people back home. You wouldn't believe it, John. Everything has blown up in the past couple of weeks. It's brought out the worst in everyone."

John interrupted me just as I started to get wound up. "Let's start further back than that. How have you been since our last conversation?"

It took me a moment to let go of all I wanted to tell him and focus back on our last meeting. "Actually, things were going really well. I was starting to enjoy my relationship with God again, like I did when I first came to know him. I stopped trying so hard to make something happen and he made himself visible to me in so many ways. I began to see things about myself I'd never seen before, like how demanding I can be and how little I trust Jesus with the details of my life. But you know what? My failures didn't seem to matter. He just kept showing me how real he wanted to be in my life."

"That's great! I know it is hard to believe, but enjoying that simple relationship will accomplish everything God wants to do through you."

"Well, it doesn't seem to be working so well right now. Everything is crashing in on me and I'm so angry all the time that I scare my own wife."

"Are you angry at her, too?" John picked up my fishing rod as we talked.

"I don't think so, but it sure comes out at her."

"Are you mad at the pastor?"

"I try not to be, but he makes it impossible. I was actually doing pretty well with him since I stopped trying to change him or force him into a relationship he no longer desires. But then this stupid concert blew up in our faces."

"Have you told him how angry you are?" John asked as he cast the baitless hook out into the lake.

"Not yet! He'd fire me for sure and then where would I be? I've thought about resigning. I even have the resignation letter typed up, but I want to line up another job before I do it. I gave up so much to work for this guy and now look at the fix I'm in!" I blew out a deep sigh and shook my head. I could feel my blood pressure pounding in my ears. "Now he wants me to lie for him."

"About what?"

"Our youth director had planned a beginning-of-school concert two weeks ago as an outreach to high school students. He'd lined up a group with a real gospel message who had done an antidrug assembly the day before at a local high school. He and the kids had passed out concert announcements over the neighborhood. It drew quite a crowd but created an even larger crisis. Some of our older members, meeting elsewhere in the facility, overheard the music and thought it sounded too worldly. When they came to check out what was going on, they saw some of the girls wearing skimpy tops and guys dressed like gang members. I think it scared them, and they've accused the youth pastor of defiling the sanctuary.

"Later we found some of the newly upholstered seats had

been slashed with a knife and initials were carved in some of the seat backs. Also, some of our sound equipment is missing and there was graffiti in the men's restroom. We had about thirty-five hundred dollars in damage and the older members want someone's head on a platter. Some parents heard that some of the kids had alcohol and were smoking outside in the parking lot after the concert."

"Outreach can get messy," John offered, still looking at the line laying motionless on the surface.

"It was even messier afterward. Some people really got angry when they found out what happened. You should have heard the battle cries down there: 'We have enough of this on TV. We don't need to bring it into the church.' 'Why are we trying to save everyone else's kids when we're losing our own?' 'The whole place was filled with hoodlums.' "

"Which would be a real plus if the goal was outreach."

"I guess that's what is becoming clear to me. It's amazing how people on both sides of this issue have turned on one another with such anger."

"If I remember right, doesn't your marquee out front promise a church 'Where Love Is a Way of Life!' "

It took me a moment to even remember what he was talking about. "It's been up there so long, I don't think anyone even pays attention to it anymore."

"Obviously." John let out a chuckle.

"You find it funny?" I snapped, not seeing any humor.

"I'd say more ironic than funny, but that's the problem with institutions, isn't it? The institution provides something more important than simply loving one another in the same way we've been loved. Once you build an institution together, you have to protect it and its assets to be good stewards. It confuses everything. Even 'love' gets redefined as that which protects the institution and 'unloving' as that which does not. It will turn some of the nicest people in the world into raging maniacs and they never stop to think that all the name-calling and accusations are the opposite of love."

John reeled in the empty hook and held it up. "It's love with a hook. 'If you do what we want, we reward you. If not, we punish you.' It doesn't turn out to be about love at all. We give our affection only to those who serve our interests and withhold it from those who do not."

"What a mess!"

"Do you see how painful it is? That's why institutions can only reflect God's love as long as those in it agree on what they're doing. Every difference of opinion becomes a contest for power."

"That's for sure. And it seems to hold on longer than the conflict itself deserves. People are angry at one another. I've been called names I'd never heard in real estate. People are still complaining about the damages, even though one family has promised to cover the costs to repair the damage and replace any missing equipment. It doesn't make sense."

"Unless it only gave voice to a deeper conflict."

I hadn't thought of that before, but thinking back I realized that those voicing the strongest opinions were divided on other things as well. "You might be right, John. We've had this underlying tension between people who think our fellowship is too ingrown and those who worry that bringing in a lot of new people will spoil what we have."

"That's not uncommon. I've been with groups who've fought over what kinds of songs to sing or who can use the new gymnasium. Some think of what might attract new followers. Others want to keep it the way they can enjoy it. These things are never easy."

"I'm just sick of the whole mess and dread going back. We're having a special meeting tomorrow night. Everyone's pretty angry. It's not going to be pretty. Some of our board members are demanding the youth pastor's resignation and are angry with the pastor for letting this whole thing get out of hand."

"How do you think it will turn out?"

"If the pastor is good at anything, it is saving his own skin. He'll probably have to let the youth guy go. He's already told him that if he will resign, he will give him a good recommendation down the road. But that's where he wants me to lie for him."

"What does he want you to say?"

"He is trying to distance himself from this whole thing by telling others he had no idea what kind of group this was. But he did. He'd heard one of their CDs beforehand and had been warned their music was on the edgy side. The pastor heard it and told Eliot and me how excited he was about reaching out to the hurting youth of our community."

"Uh-oh!"

"Yes. Now he's changed the story. A couple of days ago one of our elders tore into him and he defended himself by saying he'd been blindsided by the whole affair. He said I was the one who approved it. Now the pastor and Eliot are telling opposing stories and calling one another liars. When I reminded the pastor of our earlier conversation, he said he had felt trapped and in the heat of the moment had forgotten that he heard the CD. When I told him he needed to clarify his story, he told me that while it wasn't technically true, it at least represented the truth. If he had any idea what would have happened that night, he would never have given his consent. He wants me to back up his story and hang Eliot out to dry. He told me that after all he's done for me, I owe him this."

"It seems to me that if you owe him, then he never really did anything for you."

His words hung in the air while I tried to figure out what he meant. "You mean he didn't do those things for me? Who then? For himself?"

"Who else? Do you see how our definitions of love get twisted when institutional priorities take over? He probably cares about you. I don't mean to discount that, but he is still at the center of the conflict. Now he wants to call in a debt you don't owe.

"The problem with church as you know it, Jake, is that it has become nothing more than mutual accommodation of self-need. Everybody needs something out of it. Some need to lead. Some need to be led. Some want to teach, others are happy to be the audience. Rather than become an authentic demonstration of God's life and love in the world, it ends up being a group of people who have to protect their turf. What you're seeing is less of God's life than people's insecurities that cling to those things they think will best serve their needs."

"Is that why people can suddenly become so vicious when they are threatened? They act like angry dogs when someone's trying to take their bone away."

"Exactly! And they do it thinking God is on their side. At times like this the group often splinters into new arrangements that will better serve people's insecurities. After their bitterness recedes, the cycle will begin all over again."

"So no matter what I do, it's just going to get worse."

"Have you got a choice to make?"

"I've got to back one or the other."

"Or just tell the truth and let the chips fall where they may. It seems to me you're not being asked to choose between Jim or Eliot but between the truth and a lie."

I didn't know what to say or what I would do. Though John made the choice clearer, he didn't make it any easier. There was so much at stake and I hated being put in that position. The silence grew awkward.

Finally John stood up. "I don't know what you're going to do, Jake, but I've learned one thing over the years: any friendship that demands that you lie to save it probably wasn't a friendship to begin with."

I hated to think my friendship with Jim wasn't real. "It's just a weak moment, I'm sure. He's in trouble with some important people and is only trying to do what's in the best interest of the church."

"Is that what he told you, or did you come up with that whopper on your own?"

I stared at him, realizing that this conversation wasn't helping ease my frustration. If anything, my anxiety was growing. I let out a deep sigh as I dropped my head into my hands.

"I wish it were that easy. We've been friends a long time."

"Friendship is a great thing, Jake, but not when it gets twisted like this. As I recall, you told me that friendship was already diminishing."

Somehow I had lost sight of that when Jim came asking for my help. He'd acted so concerned about me and apologized for getting so busy he had let our friendship slide. I had been sucked back in.

"You're right, John. He has been very distant for a long time and rarely opens his heart during our staff sharing or prayer times."

"What do you think he's hiding from?"

"How should I know? I'm not even sure he is hiding."

"You're not?" he asked with a raised eyebrow, making it clear that he was going to await a response.

"I don't know. He's definitely less accessible to the staff and the body."

"It's been my experience that when people grow distant from friendships they've had for a while, they're usually hiding something. What are you going to do?"

"I don't know. I have everything to gain by backing him and everything to lose if I don't."

"So you're at the center of your world, then, as much as Jim is of his."

That didn't sound good.

John continued, "I know how powerful that looks to you, Jake, but don't be fooled. If you want to live this journey, you have to put honesty above personal expedience. It's easy to try to cover things for the good of the institution, but that's a step down a path where God does not reside."

"But I need this job at least until I can sort out something else."

"There are worse things that could happen, Jake, than losing a job. And it won't change God's responsibility to take care of you."

"What are you saying? I should just walk away? I can't imagine I'd survive without this church. It has been my home for so long and I'd die without it!"

"That's what they want you to think, but it isn't so. It also explains why everyone is fighting so viciously. They don't think they can give it up, either, so they have to win. This trap has captured many a child of God. When we're so afraid we can't make it without the institution, then right and wrong go out the window and the only thing that concerns us is our own survival. That kind of reasoning has led to incredible pain over years of church history."

"I don't mean it the way you're saying it, John."

"I'm sure you don't, but that's still the reality. When we build church life on the basis of need, we are blinded to the real work of God through his church."

"What do you mean?"

"Why do people go to your church, Jake?"

"Because we're supposed to have fellowship. We need it to be fed, to stay accountable to others, and to grow in God's life together. Are you saying that's not right?"

"So if someone doesn't attend anymore, what happens to them?"

"They should find another local church and get involved, or they will wither spiritually or fall into error."

"Listen to yourself, Jake. You're using words like 'need,' 'should' and 'supposed to.' Is that the body life God's called you to?"

"I thought so."

"Scripture doesn't use the language of need when talking about the vital connection God establishes between believers. Our dependency is in Jesus alone! He's the one we need. He's the one we follow. He's the one God wants us to trust and rely on for everything. When we put the body of Christ in that place, we make an idol of it, and we end up wrapped in knots over such a situation. Religion survives by telling us we need to fall in line or some horrible fate will befall us.

"We share body life together, not because we have to, but because we get to. Anyone who belongs to God will embrace the life he wants his children to share together. And that life isn't fighting over control of the institution but simply helping one another learn to live deeply in him. Whenever we let other factors get in the way of that, we only use love to get our hooks into people. We reward them with affection and punish them by withholding it."

A light went on deep inside me. I knew he was right. "How could I have not seen this before, John? The whole system has a hook in it. We even use things like 'doctrinal unity' to control people by stifling any disagreement. Since most people only tend to feel good about themselves when they are pleasing others, it's natural that they would want to conform to our teaching and our programs. John, this is horrible."

John just sat quietly, letting the personal discovery continue.

I couldn't believe how blind I'd been to all the ways we'd manipulated one another. *No wonder I'm exhausted all the time! I'm trying to meet other people's expectations at the same time I'm trying to manipulate them to meet mine.* I had done to others exactly what the pastor was now doing to me. I was even doing it to Laurie, bringing the stress home to my own marriage. "This underscores almost everything I do, John."

"I know it does, but just remember you're not alone. Remember how Jesus' own disciples schemed to get first place in his kingdom and to use God's power to punish the Samaritans? Until you discover how to trust God for everything in your life, you will constantly seek to control others for the things you think you need."

"What am I supposed to do then, John? Just give up my job?"

"I don't think that is the choice right now, is it? If I were you, I'd lean in a little closer to Jesus and ask him to show you what he wants you to do. He'll make it clear to you if you don't complicate it with any attempts to protect yourself—not to keep your job, not to be liked by others, not even to save your reputation."

"'He who saves his life loses it,' eh?"

"Those words are at the heart of learning to live in the reality of Jesus' kingdom. And don't forget the rest of it: 'He who loses his life for my sake will find it.' This road is rarely easy, but you will find the joy of living in his life will far outweigh any pain in the process."

"But what if I'm wrong?"

"Wrong about what? Would you betray the truth just to hold on to a paycheck?"

"No, I get that. What if I'm wrong about this whole situation and I'm just being selfish?"

"Selfishness will protect yourself at someone else's expense. Risking job, reputation, and friendships to be true to your conscience doesn't sound selfish to me."

"But how can I be certain I won't make a mess of things?"

"Whether or not you make a mess of things really isn't the issue, is it? Neither is being certain. You can only be responsible for doing what you think is best. If you make a mistake you will see it in time and learn from it. At least you'll learn to be more dependent on him than on this thing you call church. No one is perfect, Jake, and when you give up trying to look like you are, you'll be free to follow him."

John put his arm on my shoulder and assured me that he would be praying for me. "It's time for me to be moving on," he said, turning and hoisting his backpack up on his shoulders. At that I glanced at my watch and couldn't believe the time. My wife was always nervous when I hiked into the wilderness alone and I promised I'd get back to civilization to phone her by three-thirty. Even though it was downhill, the hike would still take an hour and a half at a hurried pace. I was going to be late, and I was afraid she'd send out the whole Forest Service to find me.

"Oh my goodness! I'm almost an hour late," I said, scurrying to gather up my things. "Are you heading back down to Huntington?"

"No. I'm going to hike west from here and stay up a few more days."

"I suppose it won't help to ask you if we can meet again someday soon?"

"Neither of us is in control of that, Jake, and we really don't need to be. Look what happened today. If God's big enough to bring us across one another's paths in the middle of the Kaiser Wilderness, I think we can let him be in charge of our next meeting."

I didn't have time to argue with him, so we embraced to say our good-byes and I set out for the trailhead. The last I saw of John, he was climbing up the rocky hillside to the west of Nellie Lake. If I'd known then what lay ahead, I think I would have just stayed at the lake.

# 6

# Loving Father or Fairy Godmother?

It had been almost two months since I'd seen John by the shores of Nellie Lake, but it seemed a lifetime ago. The congregational meeting that followed our encounter had proved to be my Waterloo. I had hoped my friend, pastor, and boss had come to his senses and told the truth before the meeting, or even shortly thereafter. But he did not. He valued the comfort of a lie over whatever friendship we'd had. I was shocked!

He'd given me an ultimatum before the meeting to support his story or look for employment elsewhere. I came close to caving, but in the end I couldn't bring myself to lie for him. I did skirt the edges of the truth as far as I could, saying that I thought he had endorsed the concert, though maybe I had misunderstood him. His piercing look told me my ploy had not passed muster.

The next morning he chewed me out, accused me of betraying the friendship, and demanded my resignation by the end of the day. I gave it to him by the end of his next breath, slipping it out of the notebook I carried into our meeting.

"I am so disappointed in you," he said, refusing to make eye contact. "You had such promise and now you've thrown it all away! For what purpose?" He told me he would see that I got paid until the end of the month and warned me that he would destroy me in that town if I gossiped about him. As I started to leave, he seemed to soften a bit. "In spite of this, we'll never forget the contributions you made during your time here, and I hope you will keep coming to this church to get the healing you need."

I nodded as I left, shocked at his audacity. *Who gets healed at the scene of the accident? For that you need a hospital, or a doctor at least.* When Laurie and I and our children did not attend the next Sunday, Jim read our resignation letter and, as we heard it later, launched into a twenty-minute tirade about the high character required of people in ministry. He told the people I had lied to discredit him and to take over his position. Character flaws in ministry will always surface in times of crisis, he added. I was shocked to learn that he had turned his sin into my indictment.

A few friends called to support us and say they were leaving, too, but most shunned us. In the days that followed, I was mortified each time people turned away from me in a store, pretending they didn't see me. Laurie and I attended a few different congregations on Sundays because we felt we should, but our hearts weren't in it, now that we knew what was behind the smoke and mirrors. I was lost. Some who had left the church when we did hoped I'd start another one, but I didn't have the heart to do it. The longer I delayed, the more their friendships drifted away as well.

Finding my way back into real estate was not any easier. The market was down and people were overstaffed everywhere. I started to put together a business of my own, but my old contacts had already found others to represent them and it didn't look promising.

With few friends, no measurable income, and a hopeless future ahead, I finally hit rock bottom. That was until Laurie called me on my cell phone to tell me our daughter had an asthma attack at school and had to be taken to the hospital. As I rushed to meet her there, my anger exploded. After all I'd done for God, it seemed as if he could take care of my family better than that. I seethed inside, not even sure how I would pay the hospital bill since I was no longer insured.

So now do you understand why I wanted to run when John came into the cafeteria that night? Yes, Andrea was better for the moment, but I was livid and wanted no part of God in the middle of all that. What had I done so wrong that my daughter had to suffer that way?

I'd sought a brief refuge in the cafeteria to grab a cup of coffee, read a newsmagazine, and try not to think about everything that overwhelmed me. That's when John poked his head into my private sanctuary. I hoped he would read my body language and just go away, but he kept coming. He finally stopped behind the chair across from me and started to pull it out. "Do you mind if I join you?"

*Of course I mind! Get out of here! You've been nothing but trouble since the day I met you!* But my "nice" filter edited all of that out before it got to my mouth. What came out was "I think I'd just as soon be alone."

He seemed surprised. He nudged the chair back under the table and in his gentle voice said, "That's fine with me, Jake. We can talk another time." I looked up and let out an angry sigh as he walked around the table toward me and put his hand on my shoulder. Squeezing it affectionately, he said, "I just want you to know how sorry I am for all you're going through. I really do care about you." One more pat and then he headed for the door.

I glared at his back as he walked away. A battle raged inside. Most of me was angry enough to strangle him before he said another word, but a small and compelling part of me wanted to know what he'd have to say about the mess I was in. If he got to that door, I didn't know when I'd ever see him again. As he pressed the crash bar on the door I heard myself yell out, "John, wait!"

He turned with his back bracing the open door. "I'm sorry to be so rude. We can talk a bit if you'd like."

"Are you sure, Jake? Sometimes being by yourself at a time like this can be the best thing."

"I'm tired of being alone . . ." My words were swallowed up in an uncontrollable sob that raced up my throat and convulsed me with pain. I couldn't say another word as the tears and sobs flowed from an untapped well. As John walked over, I felt embarrassed and stupid all at once since I'd never been one to cry even at my worst moments. I tried to stop but couldn't and John came around behind me and put his hands on my shoulders.

"It's okay," he said, massaging my shoulders. "You'll be okay."

I thought I could hear him praying under his breath, but I was so wracked with sobs I couldn't understand him. Where had all this come from?

It was probably only five minutes before I could regain my composure, but it felt like twenty. I managed to choke out an occasional "I'm sorry," but he kept assuring me he was in no hurry for me to get through it. I've never been comfortable exhibiting as much emotion around people, but John seemed at peace through it. He waited with words of reassurance as the pain exhausted itself.

When it did, he finally sat down beside me. I didn't even pretend to hide my anger from him. "How could God let all these horrible things happen to me when I am trying to stand up for him? And to let my little girl go through all this, and I don't even have a way to pay for it. I had begged God to heal her, provide for my family, and destroy my former friend for all he did to hurt me." The last prayer, I knew, was a bit suspicious, but David had often prayed that way in the Psalms. "And most of all, I'm mad at you! Ever since you came waltzing into my life, everything has exploded in my face. I've never been more frustrated with my spiritual life or more isolated from the church. And now I don't even have an income to show for it! Some great life in Christ this turned out to be!"

John didn't take the bait as he sat back and just looked at me with those piercing eyes I'd first seen on the street in San Luis. I wanted him to be as angry as I was and defend himself, but he didn't. He cupped his head in his hand and sighed. "I know it isn't easy right now, Jake. These times never are. Just try to remember you're in the middle of a story, not at the end of it."

"What is that supposed to mean?"

"God is doing something in you, answering the deepest prayers you've ever prayed. Yes, that process has brought some incredible pain in your life, but he has not abandoned you, Jake. Far from it! He's holding on to you today as tightly as he ever has."

"It sure doesn't feel like it. It feels like he's turned every weapon he has against me." Then, after a brief pause, my cynical side raised its ugly head. "I know, feelings don't matter."

"On the contrary, they matter a lot! But the fact that you don't feel him holding you doesn't change the fact that he still is. It just means your feelings are set to the wrong frequency. I'm not sure this is the best time to get into this, but God wants to help you see through some things that keep tripping you up."

"Well, then, I guess I'm not angriest at you, but at him! I don't want him using my life as a football that other people can kick around."

"He's not like that. I know it feels as if you've lost everything you value the most, and in many ways you have. Don't think he's orchestrated these events for some higher purpose. You've been asking to know him as he really is and that will always bring consequences. It is always easier to play the culture's game, even its religious game, than to discover who God really is and how he wants to walk with you."

"But at least I knew then how I was going to pay the bills," I shot back.

"Or at least you thought you did."

With a deep sigh I glared at John. This is what I really hated about our conversations. He could drop in a comment like that and I'd be left wondering for days or even weeks what it meant. He didn't seem to explain himself unless I asked, and I was not really sure I wanted to know anymore. I wrestled with whether to ask him or simply to excuse myself to go back to check on Andrea.

The silence hung between us for a long time. I was determined not to ask or to give him another opening. Finally John cocked his head with the slightest smile. "But you were always frustrated, weren't you?"

"When? Frustrated with what?"

"Playing the religious game. It never satisfied you, did it? Didn't you go to bed frustrated every night that God didn't do what you expected of him?"

"Not always," I responded, as I thought back over the last few years. "I remember some pretty incredible times of God being good to me."

"I'm sure that's true, but did any of them last?"

"No, and that is what's so maddening. Just when I think things are going to get really good, they unravel. I have yet to find the reality of Christianity like I read about in Scripture. I don't get it. Even my getting to know you started with such promise and now it is just as frustrating as everything else that has God's name on it."

"And why do you think that is?"

"Listen, John, if you have something to tell me, just let me have it. I don't have the strength or energy to play word games with you."

"I'm sorry, Jake," John said as he reached out to grab my forearm lying under me on the table. "I'd never play that kind of game with you."

"What is going on, then, John? After all I've done in the last few months to make things right with God, you'd think he could do better by me. I haven't got a job. My reputation has been destroyed with people I've known for more than two decades. Laurie and I are at one another's throats and my daughter almost died today."

"So you think God owes you better?"

"Doesn't he? Why should I try so hard to follow him if he won't watch out for me?"

"So that's it," John replied, leaning back in his chair. "You grew up with the idea that your goodness would actually control the way God treats you. If you do your part, he has to do his."

"That's not true?"

"Jake, God's doing his part all the time. He loves you more than anyone else ever will and will not keep his hands out of your life. Sometimes we cooperate and sometimes we don't and that can affect how things sort out. But don't think you can control God by your actions because it isn't like that. If we could control God, he'd turn out like us. Wouldn't it be better to let him have his way with us so we become like him?"

"But look at the mess I'm in, John. I've just tried to do what was right and it hasn't helped me at all."

"But it has in ways you don't know yet. God is setting you free from the things in which you used to find security in the past. They were in the way of God being the Father to you that he knew you wanted—and they were false hopes anyway. Losing them is always painful and I know you're dealing with more than most right now, but you are wrong to think God has turned against you, or that he is somehow ignoring you."

"What else can I think? I thought God was making some things clearer to me and I thought that would bring some added joy and peace to my life. I thought others would love it as much as I did. But I find out that they do not and I'm wondering myself if I've not been duped. If this was God, don't you think things would be getting better?"

"I would, and I think they are."

I could barely contain myself. "How can you say that? Are you some kind of an idiot? Look at what I'm going through here!"

"I'll admit your circumstances seem much worse now. But that's not the only place to look. You're on a new road with your eyes on old road signs. I think what God wants you to know is that those old road signs are nothing but myths to prop up a dying system. They don't really work, as you're finding out."

"What kind of myths?"

"For one, you think suffering is a sign of God's displeasure with you. Didn't Job make that mistake? Suffering often indicates that God is setting us free from something so that we can follow and embrace him more deeply. Walking in his life will always mean you are going against the grain. Don't expect your circumstances to conform easily to this journey. They will resist it at every turn. God wants to teach you how to walk with him through these things so that you can know a joy and peace that transcends circumstance."

"But doesn't God promise to bless those who follow his ways?"

"Certainly that is the fruit of doing so, but he doesn't define those blessings in your terms. He's leading you on a greater journey than you can yet fathom. Keep following him and you'll be absolutely astounded by him. The hardest thing you'll learn in this journey is to give up the illusion of controlling your own life or that you can manipulate God to bless you."

"That's what you meant about paying my bills, didn't you?"

"Yes. God will provide for you. He always has, except you don't know that. The fact that you don't have insurance or a job to lean on doesn't mean he will forsake you. The fact that others are destroying your reputation doesn't mean they'll have the final say. God is not a fairy godmother who waves the magic wand to make everything the way we want it. You won't get far if you question his love for you whenever he doesn't meet your expectations. He's your Father. He knows far better what you need than you know yourself. He is a far better provider for you and your family than you yet know. He is bringing you into his life and, rather than saving you from these things you are enduring, he has chosen to use them to show you what true freedom and life really are."

"So he likes me to suffer?"

"I hope you know better than that. He agonizes right along with you. How can he not? He loves you. He is not doing this *to* you, he is working through the brokenness of this world to accomplish something greater in you. Once you know that, even the sting of difficult circumstances will be blunted. You'll find him in the midst of them and watch him accomplish his purpose without your control. This is where his life truly begins to take hold in you."

"I think I'd rather just be happy," I said with a mock chuckle. It was the first shot at humor I'd taken in the last few days and it felt good.

"But happiness is a pretty cheap substitute for being transformed into his image, wouldn't you say?"

"I know! But this isn't easy."

"No one said it would be. But you make it even harder on yourself when you think God is against you! What if you knew he was right in this with you, leading you to the life you've begged him for?"

I had to think about that for a minute. "Then I certainly wouldn't be so overwhelmed."

"No, you wouldn't. And you'd still be able to enjoy his presence while he's working this out. You're missing what every writer of the New Testament proclaimed—even though God does not orchestrate our sufferings, he uses them to bring freedom at the deepest core of our being. If you walk with him through it, instead of pushing him away with blame or accusation, you'll be surprised at what he will do."

"But I still don't know how I'll pay this hospital bill."

"But he does, Jake! He's already working that out. The fact that you can't see it yet doesn't alter that reality."

"That would be okay for me if I didn't have to see my daughter go through all of this. I can't imagine that he'd make her sick to deal with me."

"And you'd be right about that. Andrea has her own journey with God and he'll walk her through this as well. You can't keep her from suffering and her struggle is not something God did to get through to you. But I don't think you'll ever see her with asthma again."

"Really? Why would you say that?"

"I actually came to the hospital this evening to see another friend of mine whose life is approaching its end. That's how I knew you were here. I saw you and your wife having a bit of a discussion outside Andrea's room earlier."

Immediately I flashed back to that harsh exchange. Both of us were under the same pressures and had begun to take it out on one another. I cringed thinking John had seen us. "It wasn't pretty, was it?"

"Don't worry about that, Jake. You're both in a difficult place and I'm certainly not going to judge how you're handling it. I just thought it was not the best time to interrupt. I went back a bit later to see if I could catch either of you and found Andrea alone struggling to breathe. Her eyes were alive with fear. I walked over to her and asked if I could pray for her. She nodded, so I did. Time will tell, I guess, but I think her asthma is gone."

"You healed her?"

"As if I could! No, but I'm pretty sure God did."

"You're serious? I've prayed a thousand times for that and he didn't do it for me."

"Who said he didn't? I simply added my prayers to yours."

"But why didn't he do it the other thousand times I asked him to?"

"That's because it isn't in your control, Jake, or mine! It's in his. Healing isn't magic. As we learn to live in him, we get to cooperate with what he is doing. I was just praying for her to breathe easier and have God's peace, but I'm convinced God did something more than that."

"Why?"

"I don't know how to describe it other than to say I felt her asthma leave her. I think she knows it, too. Her next breath came as easily as yours. The fear in her eyes was gone, a smile creased her lips, and she sank into the pillow with a deep sigh."

"That's why I found her sleeping a while ago. We thought the medications had finally started working."

"I'm sure they helped, but God decided to do something more."

"That would be great if it's true. I hate watching her suffer. But what you're saying to me is that I should just be happy no matter what God does or how he does it."

"That's not what I've said at all, Jake. I'm merely helping you see what God might be up to in the circumstances you're in. He doesn't need you to pretend. You've got some honest questions and deep struggles to sort out here. God's big enough to handle them. Don't run from your pain or try to hide it from him. It won't impress him and it won't help you. Take your anger to God. He knows how to bring you through this and show you his glory in ways you never dreamed."

At that, the door to the cafeteria popped open again. A nurse swept the room with her eyes. "Is that you, John?"

"Yes," he called back to her.

"You said you wanted to know if Mr. McNeal took a turn. I think it's getting close."

"Thank you. I'll be right up." Then he turned back to me.

"I've got to go now. Why don't you check on Andrea and get some sleep yourself?"

"But I'm not sure I've worked it all out."

"Nor will you in the next few minutes or hours. This is a lifetime journey, Jake. Learning to give up your illusion of control and letting God have his way is not easy for any of us. This isn't the last lesson."

"But I still don't know what to do about my job or church or anything else," I said as my laundry list of unresolved questions started to scroll across my mind. I wanted John to give me direction.

"Let me ask you one question, Jake. Is there anything you lack to get through this day?"

"I need a job. I need a way to pay this bill." I motioned at the hospital that surrounded us.

"Or you need the confidence that your Father already knows those things and loves you enough to sort them out with you. You have all that you need today; you just don't yet have all you need to the end of the month. But that's still a ways off."

"Well, you're right there," I had to agree.

"That's all we're promised, Jake. When you can trust his love in each moment, you'll really know how to live free." John started to get up from the table and I stood to embrace him before he left.

"But where do I find that kind of faith?"

"You won't find it. It's something he creates in you, even in the very circumstances you despise. Just keep coming to him and watch what he will do. He's the Father who knows you better than you know yourself and even loves you more than you love yourself. Ask him to help you see how much he loves you. That will make all the difference." Then he motioned toward the door. "I have to go."

We embraced and he headed for the door. I gathered up a few things and followed behind him. I couldn't wait to check on Andrea. As I headed in her direction, I decided I would live the rest of my days assuming that my Father's love was with me in every circumstance, rather than questioning it. Little did I know at the time how much I would need that.

# 7

# When You Dig a Hole for Yourself, You Have to Throw the Dirt on Someone

Behind me I heard the overwhelming roar drifting across the football field from the stands on the opposing side. I didn't even have to look back from the concession-stand line to know it wasn't good news for my alma mater. I craned my neck around just in time to see the white jersey of a Jefferson Blue Raider streak across the goal line with his arms lifted in exultation. He was soon mobbed by his teammates.

I blew out a sigh and shook my head in disgust. After holding a narrow 3–0 lead into halftime against their heavily favored opponents, the Ponderosa Bears had given up a seventy-three-yard touchdown pass on the first play of the second half to blow that lead. This wasn't just another football game. It was the Bronze Bell Classic, a rivalry between the first two high schools in Kingston that during its forty-five-year history had taken on mythical proportions. The winner claimed the Bronze Bell, a huge trophy that had been made out of the bell that hung in the old tower of the original high school, and city bragging rights for a year.

Nothing was more important to the seniors than to win the bell in their last year, and the alumni wanted it almost as badly. Sequoia had held the Bronze Bell for the last six years—a humiliating string that I had hoped would end tonight. The first half had looked promising, but I knew how easily momentum could switch in a game like that.

As I started to turn back toward the concession stand, my eye caught a familiar form hunched over the railing, looking out on the field. It was hard to tell from that angle, especially since he was dressed in an oversize coat and a sock hat, like everyone else trying to stay warm. Then his face turned to look at the scoreboard, and I saw him in profile. *Of all places*, I thought.

I gave up my place in line to see what he was doing. I walked up behind him and grabbed him by the shoulders. "What are you doing here?" I had wondered if this was some kind of setup, but when he looked over his shoulder to see who had grabbed him, he looked genuinely surprised. A smile burst across his face as he turned and embraced me.

"Jake, it's so good to see you. I hoped you'd be here."

"Somehow I didn't peg you for a football fan," I replied, nodding toward the field.

"I'm not really, but I understand you can't be in Kingston tonight and not take in the spectacle. I've never seen anything like this . . . fireworks to start the game and such a frenzied crowd!"

"It's a passionate rivalry. It was even written up in *Sports Illustrated* a few years ago. They bring out all the bells and whistles for this one. What brings you to town?"

"I'm visiting a few people and planned to meet one of them here. How is Andrea doing?"

"She has not had one wheeze since you prayed for her last month. I am so grateful."

"That's great. Are you doing better as well?"

"I'm getting by. I can't say everything is wonderful, but I really took to heart what you said last time, John. I've asked God to help me see how much he loves me even when things aren't easy. Financially things are still really tight, but I've seen God provide for us in some interesting ways."

"Like what?"

"I'm still working on real estate, though it has been slow. In the meantime people have hired me to do some painting or landscape work they haven't had time to get to. A couple of people have even given me some sizable gifts to help us get by. I didn't want to take them, but they said God had put it on their hearts. Each time we really needed what they offered."

"Isn't he amazing?"

"He cuts it pretty close to the wire, if you ask me. I also sold my first commercial building a few weeks ago. When escrow closes, that will be a big help."

"Just remember he's not worried about tomorrow because he has already worked that out. He's inviting you to live with him in the joy of the moment, responding to what he puts right before you. The freedom to simply follow him that way will transform so many areas of your life. He loves you, Jake, and he wants you to live in the security of that, without having to figure everything out."

"I'm beginning to get a glimpse of it. I've been reading Romans 8 again and again trying to figure out what Paul meant. It seems that Paul drew his confidence in God's love from what he accomplished on the cross. Because of what he knew about that, he never seemed to doubt God's love again, no matter how brutal things got for him. I have always seen the cross as a matter of justice, not love, at least from God's eyes. I know Jesus loved us enough to die for us, but wasn't it God who put him through all of that? If he would treat his own that way when he was innocent, how does that prove his love for me?"

"You're making a common mistake. Too many people see the cross only as an act of divine justice. To satisfy his need for justice, we reason God imposed the ultimate punishment on his Son, thus satisfying his wrath and allowing us to go unpunished. That may be good news for us, but what does it say about God?"

"That's what's always troubled me. I understood how the cross showed me how much Jesus loved me, but it certainly didn't endear me to God."

"But that's not how God views the cross, Jake. His wrath wasn't an expression of the punishment sin deserves, it was the antidote for sin and shame. The purpose of the cross, as Paul wrote of it, was for God to make his Son become sin itself so that he could condemn sin in the likeness of human flesh and purge it from the race. His plan was not just to provide a way to forgive sin but to destroy it so that we might live free."

"How could God put him through all of that?"

"Don't think God was only a distant spectator that day. He was in Christ reconciling the world to himself. This is something they did together. This was not some sacrifice God required in order to be able to love us, but a sacrifice God himself provided for what we needed. He leaped in front of a stampeding horse and pushed us to safety. He was crushed by the weight of our sin so that we could be rescued from it. It's an incredible story."

"And one I want to understand better," I responded. "I think I'm only beginning to discover how the church has led me astray."

"Really?"

I'd heard John pose that question many times, and usually it was with his eyes popped wide open and a chuckle in his voice.

"I don't think the church leads people astray. Those leading some religious institutions might, but let's not confuse that with the church as God sees her."

His use of terms confused me briefly, but I pressed on. "A few days after we last talked I got in touch with Ben Hopkins. He used to be my assistant in a home group I led before I got railroaded out of City Center. He's discovered something called house church and has found a lot of information about it on the Internet. He and I are going to start one this weekend."

"You are?" He seemed markedly less excited about this than I thought he would.

"Yes. Isn't that where it all began? The early believers met in one another's homes. They didn't build huge organizations. They didn't have a professional clergy to run everything. They simply shared community as brothers and sisters together. That's what I've been looking for since I became a believer. I've always thought our view of church seemed to present more problems than it solved.

"This is the only answer I've ever heard that made me this excited. It seems there are thousands of people all around the world who have given up on our traditional congregations and are trying to rediscover life the way the early church experienced it. Many are calling it a last-day move of God to purify his church."

"And that will happen just by meeting in a home, will it?"

His seeming cynicism surprised me. "You don't think so?" I asked.

"Don't get me wrong, Jake. Finding more relational ways to share life with other believers is a marvelous direction to head. But just moving the meeting into a home will not accomplish all you hope for."

"We know that. We've got a group of five families who want to start a house church together and really work at community. We're having our first meeting Sunday night. Would you like to come?"

"I would love to see what you are doing, but I won't be in town that long, Jake."

Just then I saw a familiar face out of the crowd walking toward me. Scanning crowds near me had become a habit since I left City Center. So many lies had been spread about me that I was tired of facing them. Now one of the worst perpetrators of that rumor mill was headed right at me. Ben was a member of the church council and we had been in an accountability group together for a long time. Just when I thought he wouldn't see me, our eyes met. Trying to be civil, I extended my hand. "Ben, how are you doing?"

He scowled, turned away, and soon melted back into

the crowd. I felt like an idiot with my hand extended and my face flushed with shame as I realized John had seen it all. "I hate that," I said, turning around to face the field. John turned, too, putting one leg up on the bottom bar of the railing and perching his elbows on the top bar.

"Ever since we left City Center, I get the same thing. People who used to be close friends turn away as if they don't even know me. Ben and I were close. I got him through a tough time with his wife a couple of years ago and now he can't even acknowledge me." I shook my head in disgust. "And that's not even the worst of it."

"It's not?"

"I feel sick when people I thought were my friends turn away, pretending not to see me. But that's at least more honest than those who stab me in the back, then rush up to me in public with hugs and smiles, pretending nothing ever happened. I ran into my old pastor the other day at a wedding. He ran up and hugged me, pretended we were the best of friends, all the while looking around to make sure others were noticing how loving he was. I wanted to push him away, but I knew how unloving I would have looked."

"It's incredibly sad, isn't it?"

"Sad? I'd say it's downright contemptible!"

"Is that what you're feeling from him?"

"I wasn't talking about *his* contempt—I was talking about mine!"

"I am, too, Jake. Other people's contempt can't touch you if you're not playing their game."

"What game are you talking about?" At that moment screams from across the way drew my eyes to the field just in time to see the football falling out of the air after another long pass and into the arms of another dreaded Blue Raider. The receiver raced untouched to the end zone.

"We're going to throw this thing away again," I muttered angrily. "Another year of humiliation." I shook my head.

"That's the game, right there! Your worth as a person is tied up in what fifty high school kids do or don't do out on that field. You're in the game and that's why you feel so horrible when people don't know how to respond to you."

"What are you talking about, John? That's just a football game. I'm talking about real flesh-and-blood people here."

"So am I. Tying your worth to fifty people out there or a lie someone tells about you is pretty much the same thing."

As the Blue Raiders scored their extra point, I knew the game was slipping away. "Besides, this isn't a fair game anyway."

"It's not?"

"No. That quarterback launching all the touchdowns should have been playing for us. He used to be in the Ponderosa District, but he transferred to Jefferson when he started high school. He's probably the best athlete this town has ever seen. Rumor has it there were a lot of underhanded dealings with the coach at Jefferson to get him to go along with it. He promised he could get him a scholarship at a major college program after graduation."

"You know this?"

"Everyone knows it, John. They even say he's got a drug problem now and the school buries it so he can keep playing for them. They'll probably be Valley champs this year."

"You're talking about Craig Hansen, right?"

"You know him?"

"I know his dad pretty well. He's the man I was having breakfast with when I met you at the coffee shop almost a year ago. I don't think you have your facts straight at all. Craig's a great kid and I can assure you he's not taking drugs."

"He still abandoned us." I scowled.

"You don't have any idea what happened, do you? During his eighth-grade year, Craig's mother died and his dad's business failed. They couldn't hold on to their home anymore and had to move in with his dad's sister and her family. There was no way they could drive him across town to play with his old teammates. It killed Craig. Even now he has few friends on the team. They love his arm, but he's lonely because few people have any interest in him."

"That's not what I heard."

"But that's the truth. I've walked with his dad through the whole thing."

"Why didn't he tell anyone? He just disappeared and showed up playing for our hated rival."

"He was too embarrassed to try to explain it even to his classmates. His problem is not unlike yours."

"What do you mean?"

"He, too, knows what it is to have former friends turn away from him when he sees them at the mall."

"Touché!" I shook my head as I smiled back at John. I never saw him sneaking up on me until it was too late. "I'm doing the same thing to Craig others are doing to me."

"Well, that's only part of it, Jake. You're caught in the same approval game. That's how this culture works. Do what they want and they shower you with affirmation. Cross them and they'll crucify your reputation, with or without the facts."

"I feel so bad for Craig now. I never knew."

"And I'm sorry for you, Jake. Religious systems, too, have to play the approval game to work."

"Is that why I could go from 'rising star' one moment, to 'condemned outcast' the next?"

"Exactly," John said. "And why you could go back to 'rising star' tomorrow if you returned and admitted it was all your fault. They would celebrate your return as quickly as they shoved you out the door. All that matters is that you stay in the game and play by the rules."

We both stared out over the football field, but I had long ago lost track of the game. Then it dawned on me. "So even though I'm not there, I'm still playing that game, aren't I?"

"Oh, yes." John smiled. "It's a lot easier for you to get out of the system than it is to get the system out of you. You can play it from inside and out. The approval you felt then came from the same source as the shame you feel now. That's why it hurts so much when you hear the rumors or watch old friends turn away embarrassed. Truth be told, some of those people still really care about you. They just don't know how to show it now that you no longer play on their team. They're not bad people, Jake, just brothers and sisters lost in something that is not as godly as they think it is."

"My daughter Andrea told me that last week at school she overheard two teachers talking. They didn't know she was on the other side of the bathroom door when they passed by.

She heard my name so she stopped to listen. She recognized one voice coming from an elder at City Center who teaches at her school. He told his colleague that I had really harmed the church and that he'd heard I had a drinking problem."

"How did she handle that?"

"I asked her what she thought, and her answer surprised me. 'Well, Dad,' she said, 'when you dig a hole for yourself, I guess you have to throw the dirt on someone.' Then she dashed off to play."

John laughed as hard as I'd ever seen him laugh. "I love it! It's amazing how easily children see through the game. Who you are doesn't change in her mind because of what others say. She's not playing."

"But why can't we see how this game is so destructive? Others are being lied to!"

"They don't want to see it, Jake. Religious systems prey on people's insecurity. They haven't learned how to live in Father's love, to follow his voice and depend on him. Consequently they can't do anything that might upset their place in the game, or they'll feel lost. Do you remember our walk through your Sunday school program a year or so ago? We wire people to their approval needs at a very young age and try to exploit it their whole lives."

"And part of that training includes marginalizing those that don't go along." I let out a deep sigh. "I've certainly done that to others. I had no idea how it felt from this side."

"Institutionalism breeds task-based friendships. As long as you're on the same task together, you can be friends. When you're not, people tend to treat you like damaged goods. Now you know what that's like from the other side, and one of the big things Jesus is doing in you now is to free you from the game. Then you can live deeply in him rather than worry about what everyone else thinks about you."

"I've been tortured by that my whole life."

"And as long as you need other people to understand you and to approve of what you're doing, you are owned by anyone willing to lie about you."

"Am I just supposed to take it?"

"You'll learn how best to handle it, but right now just know that your need to convince others how right you are is your need. It's not God's. Did you ever notice how little attention Jesus paid to his public relations? Even when people didn't understand at all and accused him of horrific things, he never rose to his own defense and he never let it deter him from what he knew Father had asked him to do."

"He wouldn't play the game."

"That's exactly right, Jake, and he's helping you to stop playing it, too. As he does, you won't believe how you'll be able to help others find the same freedom."

"Well, I'm done with it! I'm not playing the game anymore."

John chuckled again. "How I wish it were that easy. You already knew they were wrong, but it still bothered you. How are you just going to stop? Actually, this is going to be a bit of a process. Even the pain of feeling rejected is part of it. He is using what's going on around you to help you learn how to care more what Father thinks of you than what anyone else does."

"That's why I'm excited about our new house church. We can deal with real issues like this."

I expected him to encourage me to go for it. Instead, he just looked at me as if I hadn't heard a word he'd said.

It took me a moment to sort out why, and then it dawned on me. "Is this that game, too?"

"It doesn't have to be," John answered, "but it could be, the way you're going about it."

"What do you mean?"

"If this is another place for you to find your identity and to bury your shame by thinking you've got a better way to do it than anyone else, then you're sating the same thirst, just from a different fountain. That's what I hear when you call it a great 'move of God.' You're still talking like you're a competitor with other brothers and sisters. You can't love what you're competing against, and if you're keeping score, you can be sure, you're competing."

"So we shouldn't do it?"

"I didn't say that, Jake. What I hope you'll do is simply let God connect you with those brothers and sisters he wants you to walk with for now. Think less about 'starting' something than just learning to share your life in God with others on a similar journey. Don't feed off your need to be more right than others, and then you'll know more clearly what he is doing in you."

At that moment someone grabbed me from behind in a bear hug around my waist. My heart sank as I wondered who it might be until I heard her words. "I wondered what happened to you." It was my wife, Laurie. "Where's the popcorn and soda?"

I gave her a hug and realized the game was almost over. "I ran into someone and just got lost in the conversation. Here, let me introduce you. This is John, the one I've been telling you about."

"You're kidding," she said, leaning around me and sticking out her hand to shake John's.

He took it and smiled. "It's a real pleasure to finally meet you."

"Well, you don't look two thousand years old," Laurie said to my embarrassment, as she sized him up with a smirk on her face. In my recent conversations with John, our friendship had overshadowed my preoccupation with whether or not he might somehow be the apostle John.

I started to butt in, but John beat me to it. "Looks can be deceiving." He smiled back with a wink. "I'd love to talk some more, but I've got to meet up with some people before the game ends. I hope we'll have time to talk further, Laurie."

"Oh, no you don't! I've got a lot I want to ask you," Laurie said.

"Another time, I trust," he said as the crowd across the way erupted again. I looked up to see a Blue Raider score yet another touchdown. A quick glance at the scoreboard showed we were behind 24–10 with only a minute remaining.

"Don't you hate that quarterback?" Laurie said, shaking her head.

"Not anymore," I said.

Laurie looked at me, surprised. "Who is in there?" she said, probing my eyes.

By the time we turned around to talk to John again, he was gone. We both looked through the crowd to see which way he went, but we couldn't spot him.

# 8

# Unplayable Lies

I didn't have a clue what to do with the information I'd just been handed. I finally had the goods on my former pastor, but I had no idea what to do about it. If I had known a year before what I knew now, I wouldn't have had any question.

It all came out in a chance encounter at the mall. I had rushed in to pick up an anniversary present for my wife and grab a quick lunch before a one-thirty appointment. My face was buried in a week-old newsmagazine as I downed my cheeseburger at a table in the middle of the food court. As I turned the page, I noticed a woman in a bright red dress standing in front of my table. Looking up, I saw a familiar face, one I hadn't seen in a while.

"Can I talk to you for a moment?" Diane asked, almost hyperventilating while she looked around, as if the police were about to close in on her.

"Sure, sit down," I mumbled through a full mouth as I pushed my things aside to make room for her at the tiny table. She sat down warily and I couldn't help but notice what a beautiful young woman she was. Her long, dark hair spilled over her shoulders, framing her vivid blue eyes. But her furrowed brow, pursed lips, and sad expression told me all wasn't well. I had first known her as an exuberant, spunky young woman who came to Kingston to attend the local state college. Immediately after she graduated, she married a man who began to abuse her as soon as they got married. She'd finally divorced him and our fellowship had stood by her through the ugly process. That was almost three years before. Then she faded out of sight and I had not seen her since.

"Are you okay?" I asked.

"I'm making it a day at a time, but it isn't easy. But I came over here to check on you. How are you doing? I heard what Jim did to you and I've been so concerned for you and Laurie. Are you two doing all right?"

"Diane, thanks for asking. That means more to me than you know. It hasn't been easy at all. I've had a hard time getting back into real estate and there are lots of people we miss. Some of them still avoid us in public, others are passing along horrible rumors about us."

Diane scanned the mall again and fidgeted with her hair. After an awkward silence she leaned forward and spoke almost in a whisper. "I probably shouldn't be telling you this. I am so embarrassed by it and I swore I'd never tell anyone." She bit her lip and stared beyond me, looking for the right words. "About Pastor Jim . . ." She fought to hold back the sob that had already crested in her throat. "There's something you don't know . . ." Her voice trailed off.

I reached across to pat her hand resting on the table. "It's okay, Diane. You don't have to tell me if you're not comfortable."

"He took advantage of me," she blurted out suddenly while choking back a sob.

I had no idea what she meant, and as I tried to figure out what question to ask she gathered herself enough to continue.

"I've really fought the urge to tell you this, but when I saw you here alone today, I just knew I had to."

In measured words she told me that she'd had a three-month affair with Jim. During the divorce and for almost a year afterward she stayed with Jim and his wife in a spare room. By the end of her time there, they had gotten involved and he told her he was willing to give up his wife for her. She was still deeply conflicted about what had happened and alternated between blaming him and blaming herself.

"I should not have stayed there. I was just too much temptation for him, especially with the problems he was having with his wife. They fought all the time. One morning I woke up, knowing this wasn't the person I wanted to be, and moved out." Tears streamed down her cheeks.

I slumped back in my chair, uncertain what to say next. I thought of a conversation I'd had with Jim when Diane stopped coming to our congregation after she moved out of his home. I asked him if something had happened and he blew me off: "She just felt her needs would be met in a younger congregation." I was surprised to hear that, given their close friendship.

She started to get up from the table. "I haven't told anyone about this and I'll deny it if you do, but I thought you needed to know."

She stood up and I quickly joined her. "Wait," I pleaded as she backed away. "I am so sorry for you. Is there anything . . . ?"

"Please, don't even try," she said, putting both hands up defensively, her voice breaking. "I've got to go. I'm so sorry."

She rushed away as I called again to her. I felt the eyes of a dozen folks nearby staring at me. I smiled awkwardly and sat back down, deep in thought. I'd always wondered how my relationship with Jim could have changed so abruptly. But this news brought me no joy. I didn't feel like eating the rest of my burger, and the longer I sat there the angrier I got. So the one who lied about me was living a lie himself.

As I got up to leave, I found myself for the first time in recent memory scanning the mall for John's familiar figure. I hadn't seen him since the football game almost four months earlier and thought about him only with great appreciation for the things he'd helped me see. This news made me want to talk to him again. I remembered John asking me once what I thought Jim might be hiding. I'd had no idea.

I didn't see him on my first sweep and grew frustrated that he had never given me a way to get in touch with him. I had no phone number or e-mail address for him. I started to walk back through the mall, to get to my car in the far parking lot. As I passed the fountain in the center of the mall, I saw him. He was sitting on a bench with an infant playing in his lap and talking to a young man. I shook my head and smiled. John always seemed to fit so naturally into his environment.

As I approached, the young man stood, shook John's hand, scooped up his child from John's lap, and put him in a stroller. The little boy turned to wave a clumsy good-bye to John, and as John returned it with a smile, I slid in next to him. He turned, seemingly surprised by me. Then he broke into a bigger smile and put his arm around my shoulder. "Jake, it's good to see you."

"I can't believe you're here," I said. "I was just thinking about you." Then motioning to the father and son moving off, I asked, "Are they friends of yours?"

"They might be now. I just met him on the bench while he was waiting for his wife. We had a delightful conversation as we played with Jason. He doesn't think he knows God yet, but that's just because he hasn't recognized his hand on his life. But that's another story. How are you doing, Jake?"

"You won't believe what I just heard."

"About what?"

"Do you remember asking me what my former pastor had to hide when he grew distant from me? Well, I just found out he had an affair a couple of years ago with a woman who was staying in his home while she was going through a divorce."

John's smile quickly faded into pain as sorrow crept across his countenance. As tears pooled in his eyes, I heard him sigh almost in a whisper, "Oh, God, forgive us."

Why was I so excited at that which brought him such obvious pain?

"Do you know this for sure?" John asked.

"The woman involved just walked up to me a few minutes ago and told me. She said she thought I needed to know."

"How was she?"

"She didn't look well, but she didn't stay around to talk. She ran off as soon as she told me."

I could see the pain in his eyes as he stared out across the mall. After an awkward silence, he finally spoke. "What are you going to do about it?"

"I don't know. That's why I wanted to talk with you. I'm sure he needs to be confronted. It will at least vindicate me."

"How will it do that?"

"It proves he's a fraud. Now everyone will know."

"Are you sure you want to do that?" I could see his eyes had filled with tears.

"No, I don't want to," I said, with less sincerity than I'd hoped to muster. "But shouldn't someone?"

"That's not yours to answer, really. You only need to answer for what you're asked to do."

"But no one else knows, John, except the woman. And I don't think she'll do anything."

John was silent again for some time.

"What do you think I should do?" I finally asked him.

"I can't tell you what to do, Jake, but I don't think you should assume you know what's best. Ask Father what he would have you do. But this is certainly not something to triumph in."

"I hope it didn't sound that way," I said.

John shrugged his shoulders. "Who cares how it sounded? It only matters what is."

"But I want that failed system to be seen for what it is, John. He defrauded me, that woman, and those people who go there and he's getting away with it."

"No one gets away with it, Jake. He's paying for his failures in ways you can never imagine. Don't forget sin itself is always its own punishment. It makes him less the man God wants him to be and it destroys others around him, even if they don't know why. Already people sense his emptiness and his struggle."

"But doesn't he need to be exposed for what he's done? I want people to see the truth."

"Can't they already see it, Jake? After all, he is who he is, not who he pretends to be."

"But it doesn't look that way. People think he's this godly man."

"There's the rub, isn't it? When you're not content with reality, you will always worry about the way things appear."

"I don't think so, John." The anger in my words surprised even me. He was trying to take out of my hands the best weapon I'd had in a year. "He just needs to be seen for what he is."

"Hasn't that already happened? He's already betrayed a friendship to protect himself and lied to a congregation to discredit you. Doesn't arrogance already exude from his life? Why is it worse for you evangelicals when it is sexual?"

I've got to admit he surprised me there. I thought sexual failure was worse than anything else. After a stunned silence I replied through gritted teeth, "Well, it at least makes it obvious."

"Don't get angry with me. I didn't do it."

"I'm sorry, John, I'm just frustrated at the way you're responding to this. I thought this would help win people to our side."

"What side is that?"

"You know! Those who oppose the false system of organized religion and are committed to following the New Testament model of house churches."

"That doesn't sound like a side I want to be on. Have you ever heard me talk like that?"

I was almost frantic with where John had taken this conversation. "You're the one who helped me see the failures of organized religion."

"It's one thing to see through things and quite another to be against them. That's the game—and I'm not playing. And I'm all for believers learning how to walk together in real fellowship, but we haven't even begun to talk about how that might happen."

"Doesn't it always produce this very thing—men like Jim, pretending to be leaders when they lie and devour others? I'm sick of it, John."

"They are not all frauds, Jake. Not all groups become as destructive as yours. Those who treat leaders as if they have some special anointing are the most susceptible to being deceived by them. It seems people who assume or who are given the most human authority forget how to say no to their own appetites and desires. It is so easy for any of us to end up serving ourselves when we think we're serving others by keeping an institution functioning. But not all of those who do it end up so broken. Many are real servants who only want to help others, and they've been led to believe this is the best way to do it. Always separate the failure of the system from the hearts of the people in it.

"Any human system will eventually dehumanize the very people it seeks to serve, and those it dehumanizes the most are those who think they lead it. But not everyone in a system is given over to the priorities of that system. Many walk inside it without being given over to it. They live in Father's life and graciously help others as he gives them opportunity."

"I don't care about all that, John. I just want Jim's failure exposed to the world." I could feel my face flush with anger and my hands balled up into fists.

"Why are you so angry, Jake?"

I finally leaned back on the bench, let out a deep sigh, and managed to release some of my anxiety with it. I didn't really want to fight John. I wanted to hear what he had to say. My next words came out less defensive and far more probing. "I'm not sure what you mean."

"I don't know. Your response to me seems disproportionate to what we're talking about. It makes me wonder what else is frustrating you."

I thought for a moment. "The only thing I thought I was getting right was not being tyrannized by other people's opinions. For the last few weeks I haven't felt that nagging shame when I crossed paths with people from my old fellowship. That has blessed me."

"As well it should," John said with a smile.

"But now you've turned all this against me. You just think I want vengeance against Jim."

He reached out and put his arm around my shoulder. "Jake, nothing could be further from the truth. Believe me, I know how rough this is. I think you're doing incredibly

well getting through this transition. I just don't want you
to make it any harder on yourself."

"I guess I'm struggling in a lot of areas, John. Getting
back into real estate has really been hit and miss. I had a
huge deal fall apart last week at the last minute. It would
have set me up for years to come. I barely make it through
each month and am never sure how to get through the next
one. I hoped my life would be much more stable by now."

"Maybe you're looking for stability in the wrong places,
Jake."

I almost hated to ask, "What is that supposed to mean?"

"Jake, you've learned to measure stability by your circumstances and by your ability to see how things will
work out months in advance."

"And that's wrong?"

"I wouldn't say it's wrong. I'd just say it's not going to help
you walk in this kingdom. When we're looking to the future,
we're not listening to Father. Anything we do to try and guarantee stability on our own terms will actually rob us of the
freedom to simply follow him today. We'll resort to our own
wisdom instead of following his. The greatest freedom God can
give you is to trust his ability to take care of you each day."

"That's where it always gets confusing for me, John. I
do have enough for today—enough money to take care of
our needs, enough fellowship to encourage me onward,
and enough grace to endure the rumors of others. It's when
I look further down the road that I get worried. I don't see
how this will work out over time."

"We've all been there, Jake, and I certainly understand. But
that's because we can't see yet what God will do. We can only
see what we can do. You think exposing Jim's affair will fix
everything when, in fact, it will fix nothing. People who can't see
his arrogance won't be convinced of his moral failure. If he has
already been unfaithful, he'll think nothing of lying about it."

"I never thought of it that way. But I hate it that people
think he's so righteous."

"But they only think he is. It's an illusion, and while
illusions can be powerful, they are still illusions."

"But most people live by those illusions."

"Only because they want to, Jake. I don't want you to. You appear to be the bad guy when you know it isn't true. You appear to be on the verge of financial ruin, but you're not. Never let mere appearances become your reality."

"But I want others to know the truth, John. Why should they get to live in their illusions?"

"Believing a lie isn't something someone gets to do. It's something they are trapped in. You have some information that may help you know better what is really going on. Let God show you what to do with it. Don't just assume broadcasting it is what he wants, especially when you're the one who will benefit most from it."

"But shouldn't people know?"

"If Father wants them to, they will."

"But I'm the only one who knows, except for the two who have every reason to hide it."

"Yes, that's how it appears, Jake."

"But if we won't, God can't, at least that's what I've always been told."

John chuckled in amusement. "And that's the biggest lie I've heard today."

"Really?"

"Really! God has so many ways to do what he wants to do."

"But aren't we part of that, John?"

"We're part of it, but not the biggest part. We only need to do what God puts on our hearts to do, and doubting his ability to work beyond us is not the best way to hear him. The great lie of this broken universe is that God cannot be trusted and that we have to take care of ourselves. That's the lie that snagged Eve. The serpent convinced her that because God had ulterior motives, she couldn't trust what he said. By not trusting him she did what she thought best for herself. But it backfired, didn't it? It always does, Jake. Our worst moments result from grabbing for ourselves that which Father has not given us.

"We are to live on his ability, not our own. Remember what Scripture says about his ability: 'And God is able to make all grace abound to you, so that in all things at all times, having all that you need, you will abound in every good work.' 'Now to him who is able to do immeasurably more than all we ask or imagine, according to his power that is at work within us . . . ' 'I know whom I have believed, and am convinced that he is able to guard what I have entrusted to him on that day.' 'Therefore he is able to save completely those who come to God through him, because he always lives to intercede for them.' And he 'is able to keep you from falling and to present you before his glorious presence without fault and with great joy.'

"That is an awful lot of ability going to waste if we think we have to do those things for ourselves. Our biggest messes come when we try to do something for God that we're convinced he can't do for himself."

"Then what do I do, just sit around and wait for God?"

"Who said anything about sitting around? Learning to live by trusting Father is the most difficult part of this journey. So much of what we do is driven by our anxiety that God is not working on our behalf, that we have no idea of the actions that trust produces. Trusting doesn't make you a couch potato. As you follow him, Jake, you'll find yourself doing more than you've ever done, but it won't be the frantic activity of a desperate person, it will be the simple obedience of a loved child. That's all Father desires."

"Does the same go for fellowship, John?"

"It's even worse. The groupthink that results from believers who act together out of their fears rather than their trust in Father, will lead to even more disastrous results. They'll mistake their own agenda for God's wisdom. Because they draw their affirmation from others, they'll never stop to question it, even when the hurtful consequences of their actions become obvious."

"That's scary, John."

"I've watched it for many, many years. I've seen God's name attached to the most incredible absurdities."

"Doesn't it make you mad?"

"It used to, I'll admit that. But I've come to realize that

he is bigger than anything we can do to smear his name. His purpose will win out over humanity's greatest failures on his behalf."

"What does that say about fellowship? Do you remember the last time I saw you we talked about this house church I was helping get started?"

"I do—how is it going?"

"It started off with a bang, but it's trailed off since then. People only come when it's convenient, and when they do they wait for someone else to do everything for them. We spend a lot of time just staring at one another, trying to think what we should do next. People just aren't committed enough to make it work."

"If it needs commitment, maybe you're missing something?"

"For instance?" I prompted him.

"I don't know. Hunger . . . reality . . . God's presence, perhaps. It could be a lot of things, but if you don't sort that out, then anything you do together will not celebrate God's reality but try to be a substitute for it. And no substitute for God ever suffices. That's why we obligate people to a meeting rather than equip them to live in him. I've found that when people are discovering what it means to live in Father, they won't need commitment to keep them linked. He will be enough to do that."

"But don't we learn how to trust him through the body?"

"Actually, it works the other way around. Trust doesn't flow out of body life, it flows into it!"

"But what if people don't know how to trust?"

"Certainly we can help one another learn to grow in trust, but that growth is the prerequisite for sharing life together, not the fruit of it. Remember when you were back at City Center? How many decisions and policies were made because you were afraid—of people not coming, not growing, not giving money, or falling through the cracks and getting lost?"

"Probably ninety percent," I responded. "Most of our discussions had to do with our concerns that someone would make a mistake—hurting themselves or embarrassing the congregation."

"Then 90 percent of what you did was based on fear rather than trust. And you passed that same insecurity on to others as a way to keep them involved. You have yet to see what body life can be when people are growing to trust God instead of living in fear."

I had forgotten about my one-thirty appointment until I happened to glance at the clock above the fountain. It was already one-forty.

"I've got to run, John. I was supposed to meet a client at the office ten minutes ago. But I want to pursue this more. Can I get a number where I can reach you?"

"I don't have a number to give you, Jake. I move around too much to have a phone."

"E-mail?"

"No, sorry!" He shrugged his shoulders.

"You want me to trust Father with that, too?"

"He's been pretty good about it so far, hasn't he?" John said with a wink.

I smiled, resigned to his conclusion.

"Then why don't we just leave it there?"

"But I'd love for you to come and share with our house church sometime. I've told them about some of our conversations, and they would love to meet you."

"I'd love to come sometime. When do you meet?"

"Sunday nights usually. Could you come this week?"

"No, I won't be in town through the weekend. Let me decide on a time and give you a call," John answered.

I handed him one of my business cards. "I'm sorry I've got to run. But please call me." I heard him say he would as I turned away toward the parking lot.

As I did a flash of red caught my eye. It was Diane walking out of Sears, holding the arm of a man pushing a stroller. He was the same man I'd seen with John earlier. She smiled into his eyes as she hugged his arm and I was left wondering what that was all about.

# 9

# A Box by Any Other Name . . .

"So you really think this John was one of the original disciples?" Ben asked, leaning over the couch.

"Who told you that?" I asked, turning from the window and looking back into the room.

Ben turned toward my wife, Laurie, who waved me off with a smile. "That's what you used to think."

"Now that just sounds a bit preposterous, doesn't it?" Ben looked back at me with a smirk. We had led a home group together while I was at City Center. He sought me out after I was fired to start this house church. He was a good-natured tease and he didn't need any further ammunition from me.

"I agree it does, but you would have had to have been there when I met him. It was a bit strange. Later I thought of Jesus telling Peter that he shouldn't compare himself with John, even if he let him live until Jesus came again. I sort of put two and two together . . . "

"And got seventeen," Ben said, exploding in laughter as did others in the room. There were nearly twenty of us waiting for John to arrive. Some were sitting about the front room while others were busy in the kitchen or carrying dishes to the patio, where we were setting up our potluck. John called me three days earlier, told me he was going to be in town, and asked if he could visit our group.

"What do you think about him now?"

"To be honest, figuring that out has become far less important to me. Whoever he is, I'm convinced he knows the Father I want to know and follows the Jesus I want to follow. He has helped me live the things that have burned in my heart for years." This group already knew about my conversations with John, since they had come up often in our times together. They were excited to finally meet him and I was a bit concerned they wouldn't be as impressed with him as I was.

"But I think it's better if we don't bring all that up," I pleaded. "He's bringing some others with him and I don't want to embarrass him."

"Who's he bringing?" asked Ben's wife, Marsha. It was their home we were in.

"He didn't say and I figured the more the merrier."

The sound of a car door slamming drew my eyes back to the street. "He's here," I said. "And it looks like he has a young couple with him. They're getting a baby out of the backseat."

"And we don't have any other kids here," Marsha said with a bit of disappointment. "We should have let the kids come." We had decided to get babysitters that evening and I had never thought to tell John.

Word of his arrival spread quickly and more people wandered into the front room. John waved to me through the window. I looked behind him and saw Diane and the man who had been with John when I met him in the mall. Why did he bring them?

Ben opened the door as they approached, and before I could get there, John stuck out his hand. "I'm John and these are a couple of friends of mine. This is Jeremy, his wife, Diane, and their son, Jason," who was clinging to Diane's shoulder.

"I'm Ben," he said, and, motioning across the room, "that's my wife, Marsha. We've been looking forward to meeting you." They came into the room and others introduced themselves. My wife went over to greet Diane and meet her husband. I joined them after greeting John.

Diane looked at me when I walked over. "I hope this isn't awkward. Jeremy and I have been through a lot since I talked to you. John thought we'd enjoy coming."

"I'm glad you did," I said, even though I felt otherwise. "I felt so bad for you when you ran off."

"I know. It was all so spur of the moment when I saw you there and afterward I felt like an idiot. At the same time I was talking to you, Jeremy met John. He's become a friend since and has helped me work through some things and showed us that God is bigger than the failures of others."

We melted into the rest of the room and I could see that Laurie was going to take them under her wing. Marsha directed us outdoors, where others were waiting.

As we gathered by the food-laden table, I said, "Let me introduce John. I've told you a lot about him before, but I couldn't be more grateful that God brought this man into my life. We have a bit of a strange relationship since he drifts in and out without much control on my part, but he has really helped me." Then, turning toward him, I added, "John, we just planned to eat and have a conversation with you. How does that sound?"

"It sounds like family to me." John smiled. "But before we do, I want the rest of you to meet Jeremy, Diane, and little Jason," he said, pointing them out with an open hand as he spoke their names. "I first met them a few months ago and they've begun anew to follow Jesus and wanted to meet others on that journey."

Ben began a chorus of thanksgiving and then told John, Jeremy, and Diane that they should go first. John declined for them all, saying they wanted to be family, not guests. We tried to argue with him, but after a few awkward moments we gave up and a line formed. I noticed John waiting and slid in beside him. "Are you sure it was wise to bring Diane?" I whispered.

"Why not? I thought you all could be a big help to them."

"I can appreciate that, but her being here stirs up so much of the past."

"And that's bad?"

"I don't know. I'd rather not be distracted with all that."

John smiled. "This isn't all about you, Jake. Don't protect yourself at someone else's expense. You'll rob Jesus of an opportunity to do something amazing in you both." With that he patted me on the back and motioned me toward the food line and I noticed we were the last ones. After I filled my plate, I turned to the four long tables pushed into a big rectangle so we could all talk easily. I saw Laurie sitting with Jeremy and Diane. I sighed, thinking this was going to be a long night, and waved John over to join us.

The introductions continued and people pried more information out of John in a few moments than I had in two years. He was born overseas and lived in Northern California, but moved around a lot. He had been married, though he and his wife never were able to have children, and he was now a widower. When people asked what he did for a living, he said he'd done a number of things at one time or another but now spent most of his time helping people grow closer to Jesus. He also directed back to others the same questions he was asked and found out a lot about them as well before we finished eating.

Jason started to get fussy in Diane's lap. I noticed Diane had hardly eaten, and so, it seemed, had John. He got up and asked if he could take Jason for a moment and returned to his chair with Jason cradled in his arms.

"Do you all not have children, or was I supposed to get a sitter?" Diane asked.

Laurie jumped in. "No, he's fine. We have lots of kids around here, but we thought it would give us more freedom to talk if they weren't distracting us."

"I'm sorry. I didn't know."

"Please, don't be concerned about it. We're glad you're

here and glad Jason is, too," Marsha broke in. Jason had settled into John's arms and was mesmerized by the spoon John was using to entertain him.

As I was trying to think of a segue into a more substantive discussion, John said, "I'm not sure it's best to look at children as distractions. Jesus didn't. They were drawn to him and he enjoyed it. When others tried to chase them away, he told them not to. If we're not ready to receive the littlest ones in their weaknesses, we're probably not ready to receive one another in ours."

"So what should we do with children?" Ben asked. "That's been a big issue around here."

"Did your family get together last Easter?"

"Yes. We had a huge bash here with our relatives, probably fifty or more."

"When you planned for that, did anyone ask what you should do with the kids?"

"No," Ben chuckled. "They're just part of the family."

"Why is it any different in Father's family?"

Ben hesitated, so Marsha jumped in. "Because we're trying to have a meeting and the children get bored. I think we should provide something for them as well."

"Then maybe I wouldn't try so hard to have a meeting," John said, still playing with Jason. "Be a family and let them be a part just as you do at your family get-togethers. Include them where you can and let them be kids together at times, too, when you're involved in things they may find less interesting."

"But there's too many just to turn them loose. It's hard to get people to go out with them when no one wants to miss the meeting."

"Who said anything about turning them loose? Love them. Include them as significant parts of the family however you can. Let me ask you a question: do you usually eat together?"

"We often do. We think it is part of sharing the Lord's Table."

"Do you have a kid's table when you do?"

I sensed this wasn't going to be good, but the other folks had no idea how differently John thought. "Of course we do, doesn't everyone?"

"Well, actually no. Eating together is one of the simplest things a family does. If you're already dividing up by then, you're missing something extraordinary. Mix it up, and don't have families sitting together. Sit down with a child that is not your own and get to know what makes him tick. What do they enjoy? How is school going? Or grab some blocks and hit the floor with a two-year-old.

"And if you have them with you for singing or sharing, don't hold your own child on your lap, where you'll struggle with them to make it look like they're participating. Get someone else's child on your lap and make it playful for them. Do you realize the most significant factor in helping a child thrive in the culture is for them to have caring relationships with adults who are not their relatives? The best gift you can give one another's kids is the same gift you can give one another—the gift of friendship. And if the kids go out to enjoy some time together, don't send people out to do child care. Think of it as an opportunity for a couple of you to build relationships with a significant part of your group—whether they're toddlers or teenagers."

"But since they're not in a Sunday school class, how will they get instruction?" Marsha asked.

Before he could answer Laurie leaned across me and opened her arms, offering to take Jason. "Haven't you had that one long enough?" she asked.

With a kiss on Jason's forehead and a smile, John gave him up to Laurie and then picked up his fork. "How old are your children, Marsha?"

"Ten, seven, and three."

"If you have something you want to share with them, do it. But don't think that is the best way they learn." At that, he grabbed a fork and held it up. "Do you remember teaching your children to use a fork?"

"Not exactly . . . "

"But they all use one, I assume. Did you send them to fork school, or have a PowerPoint presentation on the makeup and use of a fork?"

People laughed.

"It sounds silly, doesn't it? But as long as we think of this life in Christ as knowledge to acquire instead of living in him, we'll do all kinds of foolish things. Your children know how to use a fork, but that's because they learned it in life. As they got old enough you probably put the fork in their hands but held on so they wouldn't poke their eyes out. You helped them guide it to their mouths, and when you grew confident they wouldn't hurt themselves, you let them do it on their own. Embracing the life of Jesus is a lot more like learning to use that fork than it is sitting in meetings. Children will learn the truth as you help them learn to live it."

I was surprised when Roary spoke up, since he was one of the quietest men in our group. "I love what you're saying about the kids. I've never thought of them that way. But you're talking about something bigger than that, aren't you?"

"You're right, Roary. What I'm saying will also affect how you deal with one another. If you really want to learn how to share Jesus' life together, it would be easier to think of that less as a meeting you attend and more as a family you love."

"I like that. We'd focus more on our relationships than our activities," Ben offered.

"Exactly," John answered. "And be more focused on your relationship to God as well. He is the first relationship. Anything valuable you experience in your life together will come from your life in him."

"I think that's why we really want to get this church thing right," Ben continued. "We've all wasted so many years in institutional church and have not found the life of God we wanted."

"Have you found it here?" queried John.

"Not yet, but we're working on it."

"Tell me about your life together."

"Well, we meet on Sunday evenings, usually with a meal and communion, then we have some praise time before settling into a study."

"Let me guess," John said, leaning forward. "When you first get together there is a lot of energy and excitement. But about the time you start the meeting, things get awkward. Even your sharing seems a bit forced and artificial.

When you finally end the meeting, the energy and excitement return as people pick up and leave. Is that close?"

"Did Jake rat us out, or what?" Marvin laughed. I held up my hand, shaking my head to make it clear I had not. Marvin used to pastor another church in town before growing disillusioned with the amount of energy required to manage the machinery. He'd gotten into ministry to touch people's lives and ended up as the CEO of an institution he didn't even like. He'd quit three years earlier and we stumbled across one another in our own neighborhood.

"He didn't have to." John smiled. "Unfortunately, a lot of home groups struggle with that."

"To be honest, I usually dread when we start the meeting and always enjoy when it ends," Marvin said.

"Do others of you feel that way?" I asked as people nodded their assent.

"As long as we see church life as a meeting we'll miss its reality and its depth. If the truth were told, the Scriptures tell us very little about how the early church met. It tells us volumes about how they shared his life together. They didn't see the church as a meeting or an institution, but as a family living under Father."

"Are you suggesting we not meet?" Marsha asked, sounding annoyed.

"No, Marsha, you're missing the point. Meeting together isn't the problem, but it's easy to get stuck in a way of meeting that is artificial and counterproductive. That's why it feels awkward to you."

"Yes, but we don't have a praise team or the same person giving us a lecture every week. Isn't this more relational?"

"It can be. But it can also be a less-controlled replication of the same dynamic. We're trying to get from our brothers and sisters what we're not finding in Father himself. That's a recipe for disaster. Nothing we as believers can ever do together will make up for the lack of our own relationship with God. When we put the church in that place, we make it an idol and others will always end up disappointing us."

"Is that why Jake says you are against house church?" Marvin jumped in again.

"I don't think I've ever said that," John said, turning toward me with a questioning look on his face. "That isn't how I think. But I did try to get him to think beyond it, as I want you to do."

"We thought house church was a more biblical way to do church. It offers more participation and is less controlled by clergy, less demanding of time and resources, and more relational than institutional church. Isn't that true?"

"Just because it meets in a home?" The skeptical look on John's face said it all. "That isn't always true of home groups I've been with. Many have people in them who try to control the others. Don't get me wrong—I love the priorities you just outlined and I'm convinced that a home is the best place to live them. But I know people who meet in buildings who are incredibly relational, and some who meet in homes who are not. The location isn't the issue, but whether you are caught up in religious games or helping one another discover the incredible relationship God wants with us."

"Didn't the early church only meet in homes, especially as it spread outside Jerusalem?" Ben added.

"As far as we know, yes."

"So then that's the way we should do it," Marsha chimed in.

"Marsha, Marsha, why do you love that word so much?" John asked her with deep tenderness in his voice.

"What word?" Marsha acted stunned.

"The same word that John hasn't been using all night," Roary broke in. He turned to John. "I've listened to you carefully and you haven't used the word 'should' one time tonight. Is that intentional?"

"Why do you ask?"

"I've been told all my life what I should and shouldn't do, especially about religious things. But you haven't talked in those terms at all. You seem to see this not as choosing between right and wrong but simply living in a reality that already exists. I thought you would tell us how we should do church."

"If there is anything I'd say we should do, it would be to stop 'should'-ing ourselves, and others."

Laughter flickered around the room and several looked to their spouses asking what he had just said.

"Certainly there are things that are right and things that are wrong. But we'll only truly know that in Jesus. Remember, he is the TRUTH itself! You will never be able to follow his principles if you're not following him first."

John's words hung in the air through an awkward silence. I could see the gears churning in minds all around the table. I knew what they were feeling.

Marsha finally spoke, choking a bit through tears. "I think you're right, John. The reason I follow rules is because I don't know how to follow Jesus the way you're talking about. I just try to do what's right and I'm tired of being attacked by people who say we're in rebellion if we're not in one of those blasted buildings on Sunday morning."

John leaned toward Marsha. "I know this isn't easy. But just because people say something doesn't make it so. Jesus is teaching you how to live free. Others will find that threatening, as you will yourself at times. The system must devour what it cannot control."

"That's why we're against the institution," said Marvin.

"We may be talking about two different things here, Marvin. I want to expose the system of religious obligation in whatever ways it holds people captive, but that's not the same as being against the institution. Don't let it threaten you. There are lots of folks in it whom Father loves and he will keep drawing them into his life just as he does with you. As long as you react to it, it is still controlling you."

After a few moments Marvin let out a frustrated sigh. "I don't know, John. I always thought the institution I left wasn't working because it had the wrong principles. I thought we were getting the right ones in place so we could finally experience real church life."

Murmurs of agreement buzzed around the table.

"But you don't see it that way?"

"No, I don't. If it helps, I think you're finding better principles—ones that reflect more accurately the life of the early believers. But keep in mind that following principles didn't produce their life together. We can observe what happened as they followed Jesus, but copying that won't produce the same reality.

"Jesus didn't leave us with a system; he left us with his Spirit—a guide instead of a map. Principles alone will not satisfy your hunger. That's why systems always promise a future revival that never comes. They cannot produce community because they are designed to keep people apart."

"Why do you say that?"

"Because they keep the focus on services or rituals and principles turn most people into spectators. By holding up standards and motivating people to conform to them, they only encourage people to pretend to be what they are not or to act like they know more than they really do. Questions and doubts are discouraged and people can't deal with the things they are hiding. Thus their relationships become superficial or even false because they only let people see the shadow they want them to see, not who they really are. Feeling isolated, they only become more focused on their own needs and what others aren't doing to meet them. They fight over control of the institution, however large or small, so that they can make others do what they think is best. It is a story that has been repeated for a couple of thousand years."

A few furtive eyes shot in my direction.

John continued, "To keep the system working you have to obligate people through commitment or appeal to their ego needs by convincing them this is the last, best, greatest place to belong. That's why so many groups create false expectations that frustrate people and focus on one another's needs, or even their gifts, rather than on the ever-present Christ."

"I can see those seeds already sprouting here," Marvin said with a sigh.

"That's why your meetings feel stilted. It's hard to maintain an illusion of body life when you don't have planned activities that people can follow with little effort. But you do have the chance here to discover real community. That grows where we share our common lot as failed human beings and the journey of being transformed by Jesus working in us. It thrives where people are free to be exactly who they are—no more and no less. As they learn to rely on him, they won't have to use others to meet their needs but rather find themselves laying down their lives to help others in the same way Jesus did."

"Will that include unbelievers as well? Most house church literature I've read almost discourages outreach as a threat to body life," Roary said enthusiastically.

"Amazing, isn't it? The self-focus priority of building 'our' group only demonstrates that we've missed the reality of Father's love. When we discover the power of his love, we can't keep it to ourselves. Not only will it transform us, it will also seep out quite naturally with believers and nonbelievers alike. We'll find ourselves reflecting God's life and character to others around us and we'll even do it best when we're least aware of it."

"Well I guess we can cancel our plans to go to that house church conference next month," Ben said mockingly.

"Not necessarily. Just don't buy all they're selling. You'll probably meet some wonderful people there who are spilling out of the system and are just grabbing back at house church as a security blanket. God might want you to know such folks. Just keep in mind the simplest lesson that has been repeated countless times since Jesus was here: the more organization you bring to church life, the less life it will contain."

"It just sounds like we shouldn't be doing anything, John." Marsha's frustration was evident in her tone.

"That's not what I mean. I just want to help you focus your efforts where they will bear the most fruit. Instead of trying to build a house church, learn to love one another and share each other's journeys. Who is he asking you to walk alongside right now and how can you encourage them? I love it when brothers and sisters choose to be intentional in sharing God's life together in a particular season. So, yes, experiment with community together. You'll learn a lot. Just avoid the desire to make it contrived, exclusive, or permanent. Relationships don't work that way.

"The church is God's people learning to share his life together. It's Marvin over there and Diane back here. When I asked Ben about your life together, he told me about your meetings but nothing about your relationships. That told me something. Do you even know Roary's greatest hope or Jake's current struggle? Those things rarely come out in meetings. They come out in the naturalness of relationships that occur throughout the week."

"But we're too busy for that," Marvin's wife, Jenny, added. "We try to do that when we get together."

I knew what John was going to say before he said it. "And is it working?"

"Is what working?"

"Are you accomplishing all of that in your meetings?"

"Not very well, but we're trying to learn to do it better."

"And we're still talking about an 'it.' We humans are notorious for taking something Scripture describes as a reality, giving a term to it, and thinking we've replicated the reality because we use the term. Paul talked about the church that gathered in various homes, but he never called it 'house church.' Houses were just where they ended up in their life together. Jesus was the focus, not the location. As I said, you can have all the right principles and still miss his glory in the body."

"Now that is depressing," Jenny said teasingly and the others laughed.

"Why do you say that?" John asked.

"Because we've been trying for nine months to get this right and now it all seems so futile. Maybe we should just go back to a traditional church and make the most of it." The groans around the room indicated that wasn't likely.

"What I'm trying to get you to consider is that body life is not something you can create. It is a gift that Father gives as people grow in his life. Body life isn't rocket science. It is the easiest thing in the world when people are walking with him. You get within twenty feet of someone else on that journey and you'll find fellowship easy and fruitful."

"That's what we're looking for. We thought that when we got church right, we'd all have the relationship with God we're looking for," Marvin broke in.

John continued, "Just consider that you've gotten it backward. No church model will produce God's life in you. It works the other way around. Our life in God, shared together, expresses itself as the church. It is the overflow of his life in us. You can tinker with church principles forever and still miss out on what it means to live deeply in Father's love and know how to share it with others."

"That's not how I learned it," Laurie offered. "How are we going to know how to live in God's life if someone doesn't show us?"

"That's where religion has done the most damage. By making people dependent on its leaders, it has made God's people passive in their own spiritual growth. We wait for others to show us how, or even just follow them in hopes that they're getting it right. Jesus wants this relationship with you and he wants you to be an active part in that process."

"But can we do it on our own? Don't we need some help?" Marsha asked.

"Who said you're alone? Jesus is the way to the Father. As you learn to yield to his Spirit and depend on his power, you'll discover how to live in the fullness of his life. Yes, he'll often use other people to encourage or equip you in that process, but the people he uses won't let you grow dependent on them. They wouldn't dare crawl between you and the greatest joy of this family—a growing relationship with the Father himself.

"That's what I'd rather have talked about tonight. So many groups I'm with are continually trying to figure out the best way to do church. What if we spent all that time and energy focused on the Father's love, what Jesus is doing in us, and how we can live more freely in his Spirit? Then we'd know how to love one another. We'd be honest and open and support one another on this journey. Our focus would be on him, not ourselves and our needs, and some amazing things would happen."

"But won't people who just 'follow Jesus' live independently from the body?" Marvin asked.

"Do you think that's possible?"

"You don't?"

"That's the fear I hear all the time, but I don't see it. People who are growing in their relationship with Father will hunger for real connections with his family. He is the God of community. That's his nature, and knowing him draws us into that community, not only with God himself, but also with others who know him. It is not our obligation. It's his gift."

"I've got a good friend who was so hurt by her past church experience that she doesn't want to meet with any group of Christians ever again," Laurie said.

"And God knows where she is and how best to get through to her. We often mistake the middle of a chapter for the end of the story. Maybe Father is just drawing her to himself right now. If she's your friend, stay close to her. You can be her link to the family as Father works in her."

"I have a friend in Georgia who just can't find anyone who wants this kind of life together," Marvin said.

"Father knows that, too! Certainly there are others near him with a similar hunger, but if Father hasn't made those connections yet, your friend can rest in that. It's much easier for us to find it when we live contentedly in God's provision rather than being anxious for what we don't see. Encourage him to enjoy what Father is doing each day while keeping his eyes open for others. You never know how or when God will make connections."

"But he won't even consider leaving the institution because he says he'll feel too guilty," Marvin added.

"Just keep loving him! Stay in touch with him as best you can. Share what Jesus is doing in your life and you'll encourage him to live closer, too. Don't worry about where he is right now. If Father's at work in his life, he'll be untangling that guilt. There's no telling where he'll end up after that."

"So even our participation in the body is larger than one group?" Ben asked.

"It is so much larger. That's what I don't want you to miss." John looked at his watch and turned to Jeremy and Diane. "We probably need to get going, don't we?"

"Well, I hate to cut things off," Jeremy said. The rest of us didn't want him to, either. We had a hundred things we still wanted to ask John.

"You're not. I told you I'd get you home at a reasonable time."

"This has been so helpful, John, though I'm not sure I get everything you're saying," Ben said, shaking his head.

"You don't need to. If I've encouraged you to follow him a bit more closely and to trust him with greater freedom, he'll sort out the rest. He's the cornerstone of the church. It's his, not mine. Ask him to sort out all this in you individually and collectively. He's been doing this a couple of thousand years and he's really good at what he does."

"Can I ask one more question?" Roary's boldness was way out of character.

John turned and nodded.

"I'd like to believe it's that simple, but something tells me I'll mess it up. Do you really believe we're good enough to hear God's voice every day?"

"What a question!" John laughed as he stood up. "Of course not, Roary. None of us are that good. But I think you're asking the wrong question. Let's phrase it like this: is Jesus big enough to get through to you every day? Do you think he is big enough to get past your blind spots, overcome your doubts, and show you his way? Doesn't that get a resounding yes? Share that journey together and you'll experience a body life more real than you've ever dreamed."

With that, John helped Diane and Jeremy pick up their dishes and pack up Jason's belongings before plunging through a sea of hugs and good-byes. As we cleaned up afterward and put the tables and chairs back in the garage, I listened as people reflected on the evening. Most were excited at what they had heard, though uncertain of what it would mean for us.

"He didn't really say anything I haven't thought before," Marvin said, shaking his head. "It's just the kind of stuff you're afraid to believe is true."

"Religion runs deep," I responded, knowing all too well how he felt. My stomach was in knots for another reason. As I said good-bye to Diane, she had whispered in my ear that she needed help with Pastor Jim and wanted to talk with me another time.

# 10

# Won to Trust

What a morning!

Nothing had gone well and by lunchtime I was pretty frustrated. I had spent a good part of the morning on the phone with Diane. About a month after John had visited our home group, she had come over to talk to Laurie and me about her continuing struggle over the affair she'd had with our former pastor. She'd been getting some help sorting out her emotions and felt she was ready to confront him. She wanted to know if I'd go with her.

My first reaction was to try to help her, no matter how awkward it would be for me. Initially I had no idea how to do it, or even if I could get an appointment with Jim. But the more I thought about it, the more uneasy I felt. Something just didn't seem right, but I couldn't put my finger on it. I told her of my hesitation and she had given me some time to sort through it. But now, two months later, she was downright angry at what she thought was my procrastination and accused me of not caring for her.

No amount of assurance otherwise could dissuade her and she ended the call by hanging up on me. I understood, but it still hurt. As I was trying to decide what to do, two other phone calls interrupted my thoughts. The first notified me that an important house sale had fallen out of escrow. The purchasing couple had decided to split up and pulled out of the deal one week before closing. I was set to net about fifteen thousand dollars from the sale, five thousand dollars of which I needed desperately by the end of the month. With no other deals even close to closing, I had no idea what I was going to do.

Then a few moments later my lunch appointment had cancelled. I was about to list a strip mall that was going up for sale, but at the last minute another Realtor caught wind of the potential sale and had swooped in to take the listing. The client apologized, said he felt more comfortable with this other Realtor, and was sorry to disappoint me. I wished him well, though we both knew it was less than sincere.

I sat for a few moments at my desk with my head in my hands. The morning had been a disaster and I felt suspended over an uncertain precipice. I had no idea how all of this would play out, but I was surprised I wasn't angry. I even wondered if I should have been.

I decided to drive home and see what Laurie was doing for lunch. As I walked out of my office, I was surprised to see John walking up the sidewalk toward me. He was looking down and hadn't noticed me before I called out, "And what are you doing here?"

He looked up with a smile. "Oh, hi, Jake." We met partway down the sidewalk with a hug. "I thought I'd see what you were doing for lunch."

"I suppose you just happened to be in the neighborhood . . . " I winked as if we had some kind of inside joke.

"No, I actually came to see you. You've been on my

heart for the last week or so, and I thought it might be a good time to come down and see you."

"Don't you ever warn anyone when you're coming? What if I hadn't been here?"

"But you are."

"But I had a lunch appointment just cancel, so you took a chance." My excitement at seeing him quickly overwhelmed the morning's disappointments.

"Is that place okay?" John asked, nodding to a diner across the street.

"Not really. It's a bit of a dive. The food is not great. But there's an Applebee's around the corner about a quarter of a mile. We could walk there or I could take my car."

"It's an incredible day, let's walk," John said as he motioned up the sidewalk.

"How are you doing, John?" I asked him before he could ask me.

John looked a bit surprised at the question. "I'm doing well these days, Jake. I've done a bit more traveling than I'd like, but I've met some wonderful people who are sorting out what it means to live this journey."

"Is that all you do?"

"No," he said with a laugh, "but it's what I enjoy most. I'm a bit of a handyman, so I often do remodeling work, but mostly I do it just to be with the people involved. What about you, Jake? How are you doing?"

"I don't know. I'm at a strange time. Things don't seem to be fitting together too well and this morning has been devastating."

"How so?"

"Diane came to see Laurie and me after you brought her to our home group that night. She wants me to go with her and confront Jim about their affair."

"What did you tell her?"

"Initially I said I would because I wanted to help her, but I needed to sort out how that might happen. It's been three months, John, and every time I get ready to call Jim I get this overwhelming feeling that I shouldn't. I really can't put my finger on it. She was pretty angry today. She thinks I'm just too afraid to go through with it."

"Are you?"

"I really don't think that's it, John. Certainly it will be uncomfortable and I don't look forward to it, but I keep thinking the timing isn't right, or something else I don't see yet."

"That's often how God works, Jake. If you're willing to do something but don't sense it's right when you move ahead, you are better off waiting until it's clear."

"Even if someone else thinks you're a chicken?"

"Even if. You can't blame her for not seeing what you see. Be true to his work in you and love others even through their misunderstanding of that. That's how to live with grace."

We had arrived at Applebee's and I opened the door to motion John in ahead of me. We were shown to our table and, as we looked over the menu, John asked how the people in the home church were doing.

As I looked up to answer my eye caught sight, over John's right shoulder, of someone who made my heart skip a beat. It was Jim, my former boss and the pastor at City Center. He was all smiles as he greeted the hostess and signaled for a table for two, but as soon as she turned to take him to his booth I watched his shoulders sag as he blew out a deep sigh. He looked like someone who had pulled an all-nighter. He went to a booth in the far corner and pulled out a book to read without even looking at the menu.

Distracted by his presence, I still tried to answer John's question. "Everyone seems to be doing well individually, but the group as a whole has really broken down since you were there."

"Why is that?"

"Part of it had to do with summer vacations, but I also think people took to heart what you said and have not been as committed to the meeting. People have lots of excuses and no one seems to miss getting together. I am beginning to wonder if we misunderstood you. Without commitment we can't seem to find a way to get together."

"Which might be a good reason not to," John said, putting down the menu.

"So you think there's no value in people getting together if they don't really want to?"

"Who said anything about wanting to, Jake? It's valuable for the body of Christ to find one another and share his life together. Where people are doing that, they don't need commitment. They'll bend over backward to be with one another. Where they aren't doing that, it does little good just to be committed to a meeting. I'm convinced that most Christian meetings give people enough of God's things to inoculate them against the reality of his presence."

It was a good thing our waitress walked up then to take our order, because I needed to sort out what he'd just said. After we ordered, I turned back to John with half an eye on Jim, who still sat alone. "So you think our meetings could become a substitute for God himself?"

"I don't mean it that way. I mean they can become iconic. Because people get together, sit in a room, sing some songs, and share Scripture, they think they've experienced the life of the church. If that's all been real, they may have. More times than not, however, it's just a routine they feel good about having accomplished, but in the end they haven't really shared his life at all. That's why I like pulling commitment off people. You find out where they really are on the inside, and that's good for you and for them."

"It sure doesn't feel that way, though. It feels like they're a bunch of flakes."

"Maybe they are, maybe they're just worn out with obligations. Let them detox from that for a while and then you'll all know better. Besides, just because they don't come to a meeting doesn't mean you can't pursue fellowship with them individually."

"So discipline isn't important, John?"

"Discipline holds great value when your eye is on the treasure. But as a substitute for that treasure, obligation can be a real detriment when it gives you satisfaction just for completing a task."

"Yes, but I feel like such a failure now."

"Why do you feel like a failure?"

"I don't know. I guess I want to discover real body life, but how can we if we don't find a way to get together?"

"How could they stay away, if they had found it?"

I hated it when he reversed the playing field like that. I looked at him in a mock scowl and he shrugged his shoulders as if to say, *What can I say?*

"You know what's really strange, John?"

"What?"

"I feel like I have more to teach now than I ever have, and that I have far fewer people to share it with."

John laughed heartily. "If I had a dollar for every time I heard that . . . " Then he put his hand over mine. "It's not about teaching, Jake. It's about living. Learn to live this life and you'll find no end of folks to share it with. Teach it first, however, and that will be your substitute for living it."

Our food finally came and with it a shift in conversation.

"How are the finances sorting out for you, Jake?"

"It's tough, that's for sure. We've always managed to get by at the end of each month, but this one looks really tough. I lost two huge deals this morning. I was counting on one of them to get us into next month. I don't know how I'll make it now. I was really trusting God to close those deals."

"Does trusting God to do what you think is best really sound like trusting God to you?"

It took me a bit to figure out what he was talking about since it was language I'd used without thinking. "I guess I'd never thought that through."

"It would seem to me that trusting God allows him to do whatever he desires. If I focus that trust on a specific outcome, then I am only trying to manipulate him. Besides, you've still got a week, Jake. I wouldn't worry about it. God's care for you wasn't dependent on those two deals."

"That may be easy for you to say. I've got almost five thousand dollars' worth of expenses coming due in the next couple of weeks and nothing on the horizon to pay them."

"So what does that tell you?"

"That somehow God missed something, or I did."

"If we don't learn to trust, Jake, we will only interpret every event from our own self-centered vantage point, which is invariably negative and undermines our relationship with God. Look at it this way. On your way home one evening, you have car trouble on the freeway and a dead battery in your cell phone, so you get home two hours later than you said you would. If Laurie trusts you, there's no problem. If not, as your supper grows cold, she starts to worry, begins to feel threatened, and even wrestles with the possibility that you might be involved with someone else. When you finally get home, she's already angry at you and you have no idea why.

"Mistrust will only make us feel threatened or afraid so that we'll either lash out at others in hostility, or turn it inward into depression. Growing in trust allows us to walk with God through our concerns and disappointments, knowing he has something else in mind than we might have thought."

"Well, I don't see any way I can come up with that kind of money in so short a time."

"You're only thinking of what you can do, Jake. There's a thousand ways God can provide for you."

"I guess he could turn my orange tree into a money tree if he wanted, but I'm not sure I should count on that."

"I'm pretty sure you shouldn't. But you have enough for today already, don't you?" I nodded through a frustrated grimace. "That's all we're promised, Jake. He hasn't promised to resolve our problems two weeks in advance, just one day at a time as we walk freely in him. And he told us we could be content with what he provides."

"So if I just do what I want, he will provide all the money I need."

John broke out in laughter. "Is that really what you heard me say?"

"Not exactly, but you make it sound as if I can just live in God without any thought of money. I've known a lot of people who followed that road straight into financial ruin."

"Really?" John asked, leaning over the table. "Can you name one?"

I tried to think of a name but couldn't. "You know, lots of people try to live by faith and just end up begging off others."

"So you're saying that your experience has taught you that Jesus didn't really mean what he said about seeking the kingdom first? Just because people say they are following God doesn't mean they are. People often put God's name to their own agenda. But don't let that rob you of the reality of living in his."

I didn't know what to say, so I sat back and just looked at John.

"What I'm saying is that following him, as he makes himself clear to you, is your responsibility. Providing for you is his. You'll be better off if you don't get the two mixed up."

"Well, that flies in the face of my Puritan work ethic."

"As well it should . . . "

"But doesn't Paul say if you won't work, you shouldn't eat?"

"I didn't say anything about not working. I'm talking about doing the work God gives you to do and watching him provide for you as you do it. Paul was dealing with laziness and presumption, which is not you, Jake. If he has called you to real estate, do it with all your heart and he will provide for you through it. If he hasn't, don't do it just because you're anxious to find a way to provide for yourself. You might consider that he may not be as interested in your doing real estate as you are. There are others to be helped on this journey. Maybe he has that for you."

"I'd love to be free financially to help others grow like that. I have some folks asking for my help already, but I was trying to get the real estate business going again so I could finance my other desires. You think that's backward?"

"No principle answers that, Jake. It depends on what he is asking of you."

"But it seems so irresponsible."

"In the mind of the world, it is. But if God's asking you to do it, it would be irresponsible not to."

"I guess I don't know what I'm supposed to be doing. I want to trust God like that, but John, I've been taught to provide for myself all my life. I don't know how to do it any differently. How does he provide for you?"

"In lots of ways, Jake. Some of it comes through work I do. Occasionally people I've helped in the past send me gifts at Father's leading, which allow me to spend time with people like you. It's different all the time."

"How freeing it would be to live with that kind of trust!"

"That's the trust he's building in you right now and those

deals falling through are part of it. Through moments like this he wins our trust. And it's obviously working."

"What? Why would you say that?" I asked, not at all feeling as if it was.

"Because you're not as angry as you were when we first met. You're in a desperate situation now; you're concerned, but you're not angry. That shows some incredible growth."

And for the first time I realized that God had changed something enduring inside me. I wasn't burying my anger. It just wasn't there, even in my disappointment.

"Thanks, John. I hadn't really seen that before now."

"That's how God wins your trust. He's not asking you to do something despite all evidence to the contrary. He's asking you to follow him as you see him unfolding his will in you. As you do that, you'll find that his words and his ways will hold more certainty for you than your best plans or wisdom."

"I've never seen it that way, John. I've always thought faith was something I had to conjure up to get God to act."

"That doesn't sound too healthy, does it? Increasing trust is the fruit of a growing relationship. The more you know him and his ways, the freer you'll be to live beyond the influences that tie you down to your own flawed wisdom. As you see his faithfulness unfold in your life through the coming days, you will come to know just how deeply you can trust him. That's where you'll find real freedom."

"So there is no trust where there's no relationship?"

"No, there's not. Too many people confuse faith with presumption. They are consumed by their own agenda, even quoting Scriptures that prove God will have to do it their way and end up so disappointed when he doesn't. But God will use even that disappointment to invite them into a real trust that is based on his unfolding work in them.

"I love the fact that you want to disconnect ministry from income, Jake. That's a godly desire. Nothing distorts ministry more than believing you have to make a living by it. So much of our life in Christ today is corrupted because people want to use ministry to secure their income. We have inherited systems of body life and leadership that result from people trying to find a way to provide for themselves, rather than demonstrating what it is to live in Father's care. Once ministry becomes a source of income, you'll find yourself manipulating people to serve you rather than Father's love moving you to serve them. Until you are free to trust God to provide for you, Jake, he will not entrust his people to you.

"Just don't think you're the one that has to do the providing. Get this lesson, Jake. Living in the freedom of God's provision is critical to what God has for you. Learn to live by what God puts before you, not by your plans and schemes. On any given day it could be as much helping someone find freedom and life in Jesus as it is to paint a house, or to dig those infamous ditches. He'll provide all you need, though he just may not do it the way you want him to. And that's as true for relationships with fellow travelers as it is finances."

As we finished eating, I noticed Jim sliding out of his table to leave. Surprisingly, he had eaten alone and was now making his way up the aisle that would take him right by our booth. I cringed inside, hoping he wouldn't see me as I nonchalantly tried to maintain my conversation with John.

"I don't know all God has for you, Jake. Just keep following one step at a time, doing what you know to do each day. It will become clearer in time."

As John finished, Jim walked right up to our table and greeted me. It was not the same old jovial Jim. He looked deeply pained. I introduced him to John and we exchanged pleasantries. Then Jim turned serious. "I need to talk to you sometime, Jake, if that would be possible." His words seemed to catch in his throat.

"Listen, Jake, I need to make a phone call," John said, slipping out of the booth. "Why don't you take a moment now?" Before I knew it, John was gone and Jim sat down awkwardly. He put his head in his hands and started to choke up.

I was pounded by emotions from fourteen different directions. I didn't know whether to slug him or feel sorry for him. I just knew I didn't want to be there right then. Finally he caught himself and looked up with eyeballs deeply seared with anguish. "You must hate me, Jake."

"We've had better days," I answered noncommittally. I had no idea where this was going and my gut was roiling.

"I've been wanting to talk to you for a long time but I just haven't had the nerve. Initially I was so angry that you wouldn't back me up, and when you left, so many people got hurt."

"Listen, Jim, we don't need to rehash all of this. It was painful enough the first time."

"I'm sure it was. I just want to tell you how sorry I am for what I did to you and to let you know I'm resigning my pastorate."

"You're what?" I couldn't believe it.

"No one knows yet. I was supposed to meet with the chairman for lunch today to tell him. He got called into emergency surgery, though, and had to reschedule." He stared across the distance between us. "I've had it, Jake. I've been spiraling into depression for a long time. My own doctor told me the stress of ministry was killing me."

"But I thought things were going well, Jim!"

"On the outside, sure! City Center has never looked better. On the inside, not at all!" He shook his head, unable to speak for a moment. "Do you know what it takes to keep that thing alive? Do you know how many fires I put out each week, how many people I have to prop up to keep it going? And inside I'm as dead as I've ever been. And every time I think of you, it only gets worse. You were one of my closest friends and I stabbed you in the back to save myself." He looked straight at me through his tear-filled eyes. "I am incredibly sorry, Jake, and I want to make this right with you."

I had no idea how to respond to him. I felt sorry for him and I felt no small amount of joy that his mistakes had finally caught up to him. I didn't like the latter feelings, but they were there.

"You probably don't know that my dad passed away. I'm going to move back East to take care of his business for a while. And I'm going to get some help for myself. I'm also going to recommend that the church ask you to be their pastor."

My heart stopped. "I'm sure that will go over big," I finally said with a nervous laugh.

"I don't think you have any idea how well respected you are there. You'd do a great job and I don't know anyone else to recommend. Would it interest you at all?"

"Not in the least, Jim." I was surprised at my own answer. Being in ministry again sounded good, and so did a steady paycheck, but not that kind of ministry, and not that kind of paycheck.

"Don't give me an answer now, Jake. Just think about it. But I want you to know how sorry I am for what I did to you. It wasn't fair. Of all people you didn't deserve it. If I could take it back, I would in an instant. My life was such a mess in ways you don't even know, and I was just trying to survive. That was my mistake. I should have given up a long time ago."

I didn't know what to say. I wrestled with forgiving him, but I wasn't sure I wanted to so quickly. No one had hurt me more and I wasn't ready to wash it all away with a simple "I forgive you."

"I don't want to keep you now, Jake, and I know we have a lot more to talk about before we will have sorted it all out. But I want to do that, if you will." Then he reached into his coat pocket and pulled out an envelope and handed it to me. My name was typed on the front with City Center's logo and address in the corner.

"What's this?" I asked.

"It's a gift, if you like. Truthfully, it is your severance pay. Our board spent some time last month talking about how we parted ways and most felt we had treated you unfairly. It's ten thousand dollars, Jake. It probably isn't as much as it should be, but maybe it will help ease the pain some. There's a letter of apology in there from the board, too. I was going to bring it by your office after my lunch, but when I saw you here . . . "

Part of me wanted to give it back and be above all of that. Part of me knew how much I needed the money. "I'm not sure I can accept this, Jim."

"Take it. You earned it! Maybe this will open a door to healing."

I nodded at him and let the envelope rest under my hands. Then I knew I had to press on. "Jim, I've been meaning to call you."

"Really? Why?"

"I'm in touch with Diane and she wanted me to set up a meeting for the three of us."

His eyes popped open and the fear in his eyes was obvious. "Do you know what this is about?" he asked, his eyes probing mine. I nodded and, inexplicably, tears formed in my eyes.

His head dropped. The silence hung between us for some time. Neither of us knew what to say. Finally after a couple of attempts, Jim spoke. "It's the worst thing I've ever done, Jake, and I was hoping others wouldn't have to know." He blew out a deep sigh and just stared at the table for a moment, fidgeting with John's fork. "But I'm not going to run from it. I need to deal with this." He pulled out his cell phone and scrolled through his calendar. "How about tomorrow afternoon at four-thirty? Do you think that would work?"

"I'll check with her, Jim, and get back to you."

"Please do. I really have to run, Jake, but I do want things resolved between us. And use the money," he said, nodding at the envelope. "We wouldn't put it to any better use anyway."

I nodded as Jim slid out of John's seat. He leaned over and whispered, "And think about coming back as pastor. I get the sense you're a very different person from the one I knew and they could sure use your help." And with that, he was gone.

I sat and stared out the window for a while, completely at a loss to form a coherent thought. At some point John returned and put his hand on my shoulder. "Listen, Jake, I need to get going."

We counted out money for the check and I gathered my things and headed for the door.

"How did it go with Jim?" he asked.

"I'm still in shock. He apologized, we scheduled an appointment with Diane, and he gave me ten thousand dollars from the board as severance pay."

"Wow! How long was I gone?" John laughed.

"I'm just in awe at all the things that have converged in the last hour or so. How could God schedule all of this?"

"And without our help." John slapped me on the shoulder. "Don't always expect so many things to sort out that quickly, Jake. But it sure sounds like God has answered some of your concerns."

"He's also leaving the pastorate, John, and he asked if I would take his place."

"Are you going to do it?"

"I don't see how . . . " I shrugged as John laughed, and we walked out into the bright afternoon sunlight.

# Taking Flight

The last thing I thought I saw, before my burning eyes clinched shut, was Laurie walking toward me through our sliding glass doors with a look of utter delight. It was a look I hadn't often seen on her face, especially on a day like that.

I couldn't wait to get my eyes open again to see if that's what I'd really seen, but a gust of wind had blown a cloud of smoke into my eyes and they were watering fiercely. As I grimaced, waiting for the pain to subside, I could hear the chicken sizzling on the barbecue in front of me and the surrounding laughter and conversation of the forty or so people who filled our backyard. Before I could open my eyes, I felt her hand on my shoulder and heard her whisper in my ear.

"You'll never guess who I have been talking to!" She was taunting me playfully and I had never seen her so relaxed when her yard was full of people waiting to eat.

"So that's where you've been," I said, blinking my eyes rapidly against the pain as I fought to see clearly.

"The chicken will be done in about twenty minutes and nothing looks like it's ready."

"Relax." She grinned. "We're here to have fun, not to put on a production." The smirk told me she knew this was as out of character for her as I did.

"Come on, guess! You'll never believe who stopped by!"

"I don't know. Your sister?" She was Laurie's favorite person in the world, but they rarely got to see one another since she lived five hours away.

"No," Laurie said, her shoulder sagging a bit at the thought. "That would be fun, too. It's John."

*John?* I thought as I ran through a list of last names. I couldn't figure out which one had excited her so much. But her mockingly exasperated how-stupid-can-you-be look finally made me realize who she was talking about. "You're kidding! Where is he?" I said, looking around her at the house and feeling silly that he hadn't come to mind first. It had been almost a year since I'd seen him and I had long before given up the thought of seeing him again. "He went to freshen up," Laurie answered. "He said he'd stay and enjoy the meal with us."

"Why didn't you get me sooner?"

"I tried, but he said you looked busy and he wanted to help me with the salad and relish tray. We had the best talk, honey. He made me feel as if I'd known him all my life and could tell or ask him anything. In fact, he helped me sort through some things that have hurt me in this process. I can't wait to tell you all about it."

"And I can't wait to hear it."

"I wonder if your first impression about John might be right after all . . . "

"Now you think he's John the Disciple? Why would you say that?"

"I don't know . . . There's something about him—depth, certainly, and when he talks to you, you know he really cares about you as an individual. I've never met anyone like him. He says the strangest things. At one level they are so incredibly simple, and yet on another, they challenge your religious comfort zone by rearranging everything you've ever thought before."

"I tried to tell you . . . "

"I know, but I never realized it was so freeing. Do you think he could be *the* John?"

"Why don't you ask him?" I smirked, knowing she never would.

"I'd feel like an idiot," she said, motioning to the house as John appeared.

"There you are!" John called, walking out the door and heading toward the barbecue.

"I hear you're pretty good kitchen help," I said, grabbing him about the neck and pulling him in for a hug. "It is so good to see you."

"You, too! You have a big party today, I see!"

"We didn't mean to. We were going to invite a few folks over, but somehow we lost control and people started asking us if they could come." We looked around the yard at the spirited volleyball game in the left corner, with a healthy dose of heckling spectators in the shade, a swimming pool full of happy splashers, some pockets of conversations going on in various shady spots, and a Ping-Pong table filled with food and underlined with ice chests full of soft drinks and a freezer or two of homemade ice cream.

"This is great. Are you sure I'm not crashing anything?"

"Of course you are, but we'd love to have you. It's been so long, I wondered if I'd ever see you again."

"I actually came to town to visit some other people. They are in bad shape at the moment—angry over some congregational politics that have wasted them. But Father is doing something wonderful in them through it. They said they knew of you, and I wanted to give you their number," he said, pulling a piece of paper out of his pocket. "I told them I'd ask you to call them."

"We'd love to," Laurie said, snatching the paper from his hand and heading back inside.

"So how are you doing, Jake?"

"It's an adventure, John, to be sure. We've been through some incredible ups and downs since we were last together."

"Ahh, so you must have taken that pastoring job!"

I'd forgotten all about that and the thought made me explode with laughter. "Yeah! Right!"

"Why not? Steady income, credible job, personal validation? Weren't those the important things to you when we first met?"

*Wow! That was a long time ago.* I began to think back over the four years since I'd met John. In some ways it seemed so much longer. "It's crazy, John. I don't even think about those things anymore. I am having so much fun sorting out this life in Jesus and helping others do so, I'm not even worried about what others think, or about my career."

"So what has happened?" John asked as I turned the chicken on the flaming grill.

"I couldn't begin to summarize it. Look around you and you'll see most of it. God has opened up so many relationships to us and we're seeing people capture a hunger for Jesus like we haven't seen since the earliest days in this faith. We are seeing new people come to know him and others growing in him. I rarely have a conversation now where Jesus isn't the focus of it somehow."

"And were you able to get your old pastor, Jim, and Diane together?"

"We did, and I can't tell you how blessed I was to be there. It was tense starting out, but he didn't deny any of it or make excuses. He was a broken man and offered her a painful apology for what he'd done to her. She thought his wife and the church board needed to know about what happened. He said he'd already told his wife and they were getting help. He said he hadn't brought it up with the board yet but promised he would without using her name. He also offered to pay for any counseling she would want and asked if there was anything else he could do.

"She was overwhelmed by his response and was gracious in return. I think it began a path to healing for both of them. I don't know what will happen from here, but I watched two people find grace at a place of real hurt."

"Fabulous." John smiled. As others drifted closer, he quickly switched subjects. "So are you still working real estate?"

"A little, when people ask me to help, but I'm not trying to build that business. I'm spending most of my time helping people sort out their relationship with God. I've been asked to share my story with various groups and spend time with people who are at critical moments in their own journey. I'm so excited to watch him change lives as I help them find freedom from the condemnation that makes them feel excluded from Father's affection.

"As I read the life of Jesus now, I see more clearly that's what he was doing—freeing people from shame so that they could embrace his Father. And I'm seeing that with increasing freedom in my own life, too. That's probably the greatest gift you've given me, John. I no longer labor under the oppressive guilt of how far short I fall, nor under the demanding obligations of self-produced righteousness. And I'm no longer putting that on others."

"That's fabulous."

"I never realized how much of what I thought was ministry was only manipulating people's shame—whether it was to make them feel guilty for falling short or to earn other people's approval."

"That's what religion is, Jake. It's a shame-management system, often with the best of intentions and always with the worst of results."

"But it did work, at least externally."

"Yes, but it only drove the bondage even deeper. In the end people are still addicted to shame and bounce between self-pity and self-glory, never finding freedom to simply live in him. It makes people think God wants a cause-and-effect relationship with them. If they'll be good, he'll be good to them."

"I'm now seeing that's why so many people live alienated from him. I visited two terminally ill people in the last month and both of them were distraught over the idea that they had done something wrong to deserve their illnesses, though they weren't sure what. It took a long time to get beneath the surface of their pat answers, but they both finally admitted how angry they were at God for not healing them and full of guilt for having such thoughts."

"Most never own up to that anger because they're afraid something worse will happen to them. So they go on feeling as if God is unfair to them and they are never able to resolve that—sort of like you were in the hospital that night."

"I remember it well, John. I love how God has been changing

me. Sometimes I don't even notice he's doing it until I'm in a situation and I watch myself respond in ways I never would have before. I am enjoying the Jake he is allowing to emerge."

"Just like a butterfly taking wing from its cocoon, Jake. Isn't it sad that we thought we could press people into spiritual change, instead of helping them grow to trust Father more and find him changing them? You can't press a caterpillar into a butterfly mold and make it fly. It has to be transformed from the inside."

"And it is so much more exciting lifting shame off people than burdening them down with it. No wonder Christian fellowship has to be sold as an obligation. Who would want to hang out with people who are always laying a guilt trip on you or pressuring you to meet their expectations?"

"Which is why body life often ends up so performance-based and manipulative. Isn't this so much better?" John said, surveying the yard.

I wasn't sure what he meant by that but nodded in agreement. "I've even started posting the story of our conversations on a Web site, John. I hope you don't mind. The response has been incredible. People all over the world have been on similar journeys, rethinking their lives in him and what lives as his church can be. It seems that many people are seeing through the emptiness of religious form. I've lost count of the people who have told me that my story reflects theirs in so many ways, except for you of course. One guy was even upset that in all his desperation to sort out God's life, he hadn't met you if you were still a—" *Oops!* I thought it best not to finish that sentence.

But John wouldn't let me off so easily. "Still what, Jake? What have you told them?"

"I left it open that you might be John, the disciple of Jesus. You know I wondered that in the beginning, so I've been honest about that."

"And what conclusion have you come to?" John looked up with a smirk.

"I don't know. Jesus told Peter that it was possible. And you'll have to admit, some incredible things have happened in my life since we met. You seem to have a grip on this journey like no one I've met before. You've confirmed some of my deepest hopes and helped me live them more freely. The question of who you are has honestly become far less important to me. But I'll admit to being curious. And you've never denied it."

John smiled, and just as he opened his mouth we were interrupted. Marvin came over and threw his arms around John from behind. "Look who's here!"

John turned around and smiled. "Marvin, isn't it?"

"You remembered? That's amazing. I saw you over here with Jake and thought I'd get in on the action. No one told me you were coming."

"They didn't know, either. I just happened by. You were a pastor at one time, too, weren't you?"

"I won't focus on your sins if you won't focus on mine." Marvin laughed.

"You can focus on mine, if you like. It just leaves me more in awe of him," John answered.

Marvin laughed awkwardly, as if he couldn't quite find the joke that surely had to be there. After a bit more banter between them, John turned back to me.

"I notice quite a few people are here from that home group. How is that going, Jake?"

"There isn't much 'that' to talk about, John. We've never gotten back to any kind of regular meeting since your visit. I don't know why, really, but the relationships have grown and we see one another often. It hasn't bothered me, but sometimes I wonder if it should."

"Well, it bothers me," Marvin said.

"And why is that?" John asked.

"Because I don't feel like I'm doing anything that counts."

"Such as . . . "

"I don't know. That's the funny part," Marvin said, shaking his head and sighing in frustration. "I've never had more fruitful relationships and I'm seeing people from my own neighborhood and at work open their lives to Jesus. It seems I'm with people all the time."

"And that's not productive?"

"I don't know if 'productive' is the right word. It just doesn't seem focused somehow. Some folks I know aren't finding fellowship like I have. They seem adrift without the focus that regular fellowship provides. If our old group was meeting, I'd invite them."

"And what would that change?" John asked.

"I don't know. I think it would anchor them somehow to a group." It looked like Marvin expected John to answer, and when he didn't, the awkwardness kept him going. "They need something." He paused again, but John still wasn't biting. "Some identity, I guess."

"Would a meeting provide that, or would it simply mask the lack of it?" John asked.

I just kept turning the sizzling chicken, grateful I wasn't the one being grilled this time.

"My hope would be that it would provide focus and motivation."

"So that comes from a meeting?" John asked.

Marvin just looked at John with a confused look on his face. I'm not sure he knew what to say, or perhaps he was trying John's technique of waiting him out with silence.

"It would help, wouldn't it?" Marvin finally blurted out a bit frustrated.

John put his arm around Marvin's shoulders. "I am not trying to frustrate you. But it is important that you think these things through. If you're going to have a meeting to hopefully provide some focus, it will probably turn out to be more distracting than helpful. People will come to the meeting thinking that's their focus and in time it will prove insufficient for that."

"Why?" Marvin's tone had softened a bit.

"Because it is knowing Father that provides the motivation. Meetings are a poor substitute for that."

"So we just sit around and do nothing?" Marvin's frustration resurfaced.

"Who said anything about doing nothing? I am only encouraging you not to start a meeting just to start a meeting. Every time people see God moving, someone has to build a building or start a movement. Peter was that way at the Transfiguration. When he couldn't think of anything else to do, he proposed a building program. If you're going to walk this way, Marvin, you've got to find freedom from the overestimation of your own capabilities."

"My what?" Marvin laughed. "I don't even know what that means."

"It means that the work of building the church is his, not yours or mine. Don't think you can put something together by your own ingenuity. That has been tried a zillion times in the last two thousand years, always with the same results. Sure, it's fun initially, and the excitement of seeing God touch lives overshadows our own attempts to organize it. But that doesn't last forever. Eventually people end up cemented into that which is designed to protect God's life among them. But it often ends up shoving him out in deference to their own wisdom. We're just not bright enough to control the ways in which God works."

"Nor would I want to," Marvin answered.

John smiled. "Which is why we're having this conversation . . . "

"But what is the church, John, if it's not getting together regularly?"

"I'm not saying it can't meet, Marvin. I'm just saying that meetings won't accomplish what you're looking for. Look around you." John's hand swept the backyard. "Aren't people together all over?"

"You're calling this a church, John?" Marvin was as surprised as I was.

"Yeah! I thought it was a barbecue," I added.

"No, I'm saying the church is here. Here are people who love him. Over the course of this day they will share a lot of his life together, I'm sure. Jesus said it only takes two or three and he never said anything about having to do it at the same time, same place, same way every week. He didn't seem to think of the church as something we do at all, or even go to, but a reality we live in every day.

"Don't you see you're already doing it? Living as his body, we will encourage one another daily and stimulate one another to love more deeply and to live more graciously. It can be as simple as having a barbecue."

"Even without worship or Bible study?" Marvin asked.

"We're already talking about how Father works, aren't we? And worship isn't having a song service or prayer time, Marvin. It's living as a daily sacrifice in the life of Jesus, which is letting him demonstrate his reality through you. This is the joy of living in the kingdom—watching him work in you. But I'm sure if someone here wants to pull together some people to sing, praise, or pray, others would want to, too, and it would be awesome. It looks like those people over there are praying." John pointed to a group on the patio who were holding hands in a circle.

"But it's not what we learned to call 'church.'"

"Of course not! It can't be this easy. It can't be this much fun. We have to work at it more, be more miserable. Don't you see that's how the life of the kingdom is snatched from your hearts?" John shook his head with a sigh. "There will be trouble enough as you move along in this world. Wouldn't you rather share life together as believers with joy and encouragement?"

"But how will new believers grow, John? Don't we need teaching?"

"What are we doing now? I'm trying to help you discover something that will set you free in ways you can't even imagine. Isn't that teaching?"

"But not everyone's involved. Some are missing out."

"They might be missing this conversation, but I doubt they are missing out on what God wants to do in them today. He's pretty good at that."

"Are you saying it is better not to have a meeting?"

"It's not a matter of what's better. It's a matter of what's real. There are lots of ways the church can celebrate its life together. At the moment you only seem to grasp one of them. Seeing the church as a reality instead of an activity will allow you to celebrate the church however she expresses herself around you. I wouldn't say this is better. But it certainly isn't worse. Lots of incredible things will happen today because you're together.

"Sometimes that life is best expressed in a conversation like this. Sometimes it's best expressed in a larger conversation that a meeting might facilitate. When you can only see it one way, you miss so many other ways in which Father works. Instead of thinking about what kind of meeting or group we should have, ask what would help people best grow in his life. Jake had some good thoughts on that a few minutes ago."

"What?" I said, pulling the last of the chicken off the grill. I was unsure what John was referring to. "We weren't talking about the church, were we?"

"Sure we were. People learning to live in relationship to Father in freedom from shame is the core of body life. Find out how to share that life and you'll be the body."

Marvin was set to ask another question, but I picked up the platter of chicken and motioned them to follow me over to where the rest of the food had been laid out and people were gathering. I welcomed everyone, made reference to John joining us, and asked if he would pray for us. He smiled back at me, paused a minute, scanned the table, and then nodded.

"Let's all get an empty cup," John said, taking a stack of paper cups and passing them to those nearby. Then he picked up a loaf of bread sitting at the table. He started to tear the bread into chunks and passed it to those near him. "Everyone grab a piece." Then, with a wink at Laurie, he picked up a pitcher of grape juice she had just put on the counter by the window. He poured a few cups near him and handed the pitcher to Jeremy to pour the rest. As soon as everyone had some, John lifted up the bread in his hand and others followed his lead. John thanked God for all his provision, from the food on the table, to forgiveness of sin, to good friends, and above all for life in the Son.

"His body was broken that your spirits might be alive. Think about that and him as you eat." And we all did so. Then John held up his cup. "This is the blood of his covenant that cleanses us from sin and refreshes our spirits. This is the last meal he ate that night with his followers, and he promised we would do it again in the age that is coming.

"To our King, our Redeemer and older Brother in Father's house," John said, lifting his cup and pausing briefly. Others quickly joined the toast expressing their gratefulness to Jesus.

Finally John finished. "Until we see you face-to-face," he said, looking upward. Then he turned to acknowledge those near him with a tap of his cup to theirs. And then we drank together and stood in silence, awed by his grace and our love for one another. Eventually the silence gave way to some hugs and finally a line formed for the food.

After we filled our plates, our conversation with John continued with a number of others who joined us on the patio. After some introductions, Marvin took us back to where we left off. "I love your view of the church, John, but do we do this every week?"

"How about it, Jake?"

"Only if we have it at Marvin's house and let him cook," I suggested.

"It might help you to not think about what you do every week, but rather about what Jesus is asking you to do today. You obviously have a heart for people you feel are being overlooked. That's fabulous. But don't think in terms of a routine to motivate them, but what Jesus is asking you to do to encourage or equip them. It's that simple."

"Like inviting them over to dinner."

"Yes, or even to invite some to a study together if that's on your heart."

"That's what I've wanted to do, but I felt like that might be weird."

"What if you just invited some of those people to your house for a six-week study on some facet of our life in God? I think some people would jump at that."

"What do I do when that's over?"

"Whatever he gives you to do next. Remember, equip people to live in him first; then you'll see how he brings his body together. Don't get me wrong. I love it when a group of Christians want to intentionally walk together as an expression of community—listening to God together, sharing their lives and resources, encouraging and caring for one another, and doing whatever else God might ask them to do. But you can't organize that with people who aren't ready. Remember, discipleship always comes before community. When you learn to follow Jesus yourself and help others to do the same, you'll find body life springing up all around you."

"But what does that look like?"

"It can look like anything. I know people who meet for hikes in the woods and breakfast under the trees. I know families that have moved to the same neighborhood together so they can enjoy greater proximity to one another. I know some really healthy house churches that live out a shared life together and those who meet in larger buildings. I know others who work on a team together to build houses for the poor, cook at a mission, or some other creative way to let the life of Jesus be known in their culture.

"It can look like a hundred different things because Father is so creative. Try to copy any of them and you'll find it turns lifeless and empty after the initial excitement of starting something new fades away. The church thrives where people are focused on Jesus, not where they are focused on church.

"This is a great time to learn to enjoy him together. Just keep living, loving, and listening, and he will lead you to whatever expression of church life best fits his plans. Don't be concerned if it's nothing you can point to and say, 'That is the church.' You are the church. Don't be afraid to live in that reality."

"If church can be this simple, John, how do leaders fit in all of this? Don't we need elders and pastors and apostles?"

"For what?"

"Doesn't someone need to be in charge and organize things so people will know what to do?" Marvin was almost beside himself. I cringed inside, knowing he wasn't going to hear what he wanted.

"Why, so people can follow someone else instead of following Jesus? Don't you see we already have a leader? The church gives Jesus first place in everything and it will refuse to let anyone else crawl up in his seat."

"So leaders aren't important either?"

"Not the way you've been taught to think of them. One can hardly conceive of body life today without an organization and a leader shaping others with his vision. Some love to lead; others desperately want to be led. This system has made God's people so passive most can't even imagine living without a human leader to identify with. Then we wonder why our spirituality falls so painfully short. Read through the New Testament again and you'll find there is very little focus on anything like leadership as we've come to think of it today."

"But there were elders and apostles and pastors, weren't there?"

"There were, but they weren't out front leading people after their personal visions. They were behind the scenes doing exactly what you have on your heart to do, Marvin—helping people to live deeply in Christ so that he can lead them! Elders won't end up managing machinery but equipping followers by helping them find a real relationship with the living God. That's why he asked us to help people become his disciples and why he said he would build his church. Let's focus on our task and let him do his."

"But where do we find this kind of leader today?"

"Don't look for leaders as you've come to think of them. Think of brothers and sisters who are a bit farther along the journey than you are. They're all around you—in this city and this yard."

"But how do we know who they are if they're not designated?"

"My question would be, how do we know if they really are servant leaders just because they have a title? Haven't you known many so-called pastors or elders who didn't have the spiritual maturity to back it up? Didn't Jesus tell us that those who facilitate within this family are not those who exercise authority over others, but those who serve? Is it really that difficult to tell who they are?" John asked.

"I think I'd prefer name badges," Marvin said, and we all laughed.

Just then a middle-aged single mom was walking behind me to join some others out on the grass. As I nodded and smiled, she paused and spoke to me quietly. "Could I ask you something, Jake?"

"Of course, Christie."

"I'm worried about my car," she said. "It made some strange noise coming over here and I'd feel better if someone could check it out for me."

"I'd be happy to, but I really don't know that much about it. Do you know Buck over there in the blue shirt?" I said, pointing.

She looked and nodded. "Not well, but I've met him."

"He knows more about cars than anyone here. I'll ask him to check it out for you."

"That'd be great," she said, moving on to join some others.

As I turned back I realized the others had been listening to our conversation and John was looking right at me. "It's as simple as that," John said, with an open hand gesturing to me.

None of us knew what he was talking about. Our awkward silence demonstrated that. "Why did Jake send Christie to Buck?"

"He's a car guy," one of the others said. "Everyone knows that. It's his passion."

"I don't think Christie did, and Jake just pointed him out. Finding God's gifts in the family can be that simple. Jesus will give you relationships to pursue. As you grow in them, you'll know what he's gifted others to do. It's not so clandestine that most people won't know it. And when you find someone who doesn't recognize gifts in others, you can help them by pointing them out. That may have been all Paul asked Timothy and Titus to do. They certainly weren't appointing management teams. Couldn't they have just identified those who knew the truth of the gospel and had been changed by it? Others who claimed to be weren't, and Paul didn't want young believers confused by them."

"And that works?" Marvin asked, shaking his head.

"Better than anything else I know," John answered. "We can trust Jesus with this! He's a far better manager of church life than any of us will ever be. Live in him and follow whatever he puts on your heart to do and you'll be awed by what he does among you."

"People think we're odd already," Laurie added.

With a good laugh, John stood up and apologized for having to leave. People groaned, hoping they could ask him some more questions.

"Can we do this again?" Marvin asked.

"I'd love to if it works out, but that's not my decision."

"But we have so many other things we would love to ask!" someone else added.

"Then ask Jesus," John responded. "I could answer questions all day and it wouldn't make a difference. This life can't be neatly sewn up in the intellect. It must be uncovered in the journey. He'll make things clear to you as you need them."

With that he tossed his plate in the garbage can and headed out the side gate.

# 12

# The Great Gathering

It had been a long time since I stood on a stage sharing with a roomful of people neatly lined up in rows. I felt strange accepting the invitation and even more awkward going through with it. But Bryce, the pastor of Cornerstone Chapel, had invited me to speak to his congregation about my growing relationship of trust with the Father.

I had only known Bryce at a distance through some ministerial meetings years back, so his call two months before caught me off-guard. He said he'd heard some rumors and wanted to get together and hear from me firsthand. I could only imagine what he'd heard or why he cared, but I thought it would be fun to find out. One lunch appointment had become several as I discovered he was struggling with the same frustrations about his life in Christ that I had years before.

Nothing could have shocked me more. He was a youth pastor when I had known him and since had become the senior pastor. His congregation was growing rapidly as people came from two other large fellowships that were hemorrhaging after their popular pastors had left, one for a larger congregation and the other in a cloud of scandal. Bryce's engaging and humorous speaking style, blended with musicians that rivaled professionals anywhere, made Cornerstone the hottest place for evangelicals to be seen. They already had three services in a large facility and were considering a building program. I would have thought that Bryce would have been tickled to death.

Not so—at least about the tickled part. At our first meeting he told me he was dying spiritually and was concerned that most of his people were, too. His relationship with God was being swallowed up by the demands of a growing congregation. "I'm coming to the conclusion that there is no correlation between the success of my ministry and the fruitfulness of my own relationship with him. In fact, I seem to preach my best sermons in the midst of my worst failures. I am beginning to think ministry is where I hide from him."

He wanted to recapture the passion for God that had pointed him toward ministry originally but didn't know how to get there. When he expressed that hunger to others, they assured him that the wave of fruitfulness he was riding was proof of God's blessing and he should ignore his doubts. That would work for a while, but his inner loneliness and struggle with ever-increasing temptation would eventually win the day and drive him toward anger and depression, most of which he'd take out unseen on his family at home.

Neither of us had any idea where this might lead, but we both knew he was taking a risk with the track he was on. But he kept saying that he didn't want to settle for anything less than a real relationship with God, regardless of what it would cost him. He had even asked me to share with his congregation at their weekend services.

The service was over. Laurie and I had just said our good-byes to Bryce and walked toward the parking lot squinting in the bright afternoon sun. A few people thanked me for coming.

Then I saw him. It was John walking out of the parking lot with what looked like a mischievous smile on his face. We embraced and Laurie seemed more thrilled than I to see him. I'll have to admit I felt a bit embarrassed to be standing there.

"What are you doing here?" I asked him. "Oh, let me guess," I added mockingly. "You just fell out of the sky into this parking lot and saw me here."

"No. It's not nearly as fancy as all that. I spent the night with Diane and Jeremy. As I glanced through their newspaper I saw you were speaking here and wanted to see you. They let me off a few moments ago. They are doing really well, aren't they?"

"That's an understatement. I've never seen two people grow so quickly. We're having a great time walking this out with them."

"They told me that they had even been in touch with Jim and his wife again. I love when God brings real reconciliation even through betrayal and tragedy."

"It's a great story," Laurie interjected, "but I wonder why they didn't tell us you were coming to town."

"They had no idea." He smiled, and I knew what that meant.

I asked him if we could take him to lunch, but he said he didn't have the time. Someone from Los Angeles was going to meet him in a few moments. "Let's talk here as long as we can," John said motioning to a picnic table under the trees at the edge of the parking lot. As we walked over, I heard the call of some geese above me and looked up to see a dozen of them in V formation headed south. It was a breathtaking fall day. Then I heard another flock behind me.

"So what are you doing here?" John asked.

"You caught me!" I threw up my hands in mock surrender, "consorting with the enemy."

"You don't really think that," John laughed. "At least I hope not."

"No, I don't. But as I prepared for this, I wondered what you would think about my being here. Some people talk about these institutions like the Egyptian bondage of the Israelites. I didn't know if you fell into that camp."

"Not exactly," John answered with a smile. "So how did this come about?"

I caught John up on my relationship with Bryce and his invitation to come and speak.

"So how did it go?" John asked.

"You'd have to ask some of them."

"It was wonderful," Laurie added. "He had them laughing one moment and crying the next as he talked about living in Father's love."

"But it was very awkward for me, John. I used to love those settings, but it seemed so ineffective today."

"How so?"

"I've done it for years, but I'm not sure how valuable it is in helping people learn to live free. I've no doubt you can plant some seeds that way, and there is the rare moment when a light really comes on for someone. But most people get tone deaf to it after a while. Even when they hear something that hits them hard, they forget about it when they go back to their lives. On the other hand, my conversations with you have been life-changing. And I know it wasn't just the words you spoke, but when you spoke them. It was in the moment of struggle trying to answer my questions or posing your own that made them so powerful. I just don't know how to replicate that in a sermon."

"You can't, of course, but that doesn't mean what you did today was worthless. All things have their place, but as you say, this isn't first place. Over the long haul, systems like these don't help people learn to live deeply in the life of Jesus or experience the depths of Christian community. But they often introduce people to the fact that God exists."

"I know I got some truth and my hunger for God in a congregation just like this," Laurie commented.

"But did it also satisfy that hunger, Laurie?"

"At times I thought it did. Looking back, however, I think it only frustrated me. It made me hungry to know God in a way that it could not fulfill. But it also made me feel that was my fault. I felt like I didn't understand enough or wasn't working hard enough."

"That's what happens when an institution tries to do what it cannot do. By providing services to keep people coming, it unwittingly becomes a distraction to real spiritual life. It offers an illusion of spirituality in highly orchestrated experiences, but it cannot show people how to live each day in him through the real struggles of life.

"That's one of the strangest things about Christianity locking itself into an institutional box. Who would choose to be raised in an orphanage? Our hearts hunger for family. That's where children learn who they are and how they fit into the world. This is like an orphanage revolving around the convenience of the whole. You survive best in it by following its rules, but that's not how Jesus connects you with his Father. For that you need a family and brothers and sisters who can respond to you in the moment, not wait for a meeting or to schedule a seminar."

"That's how you've helped me so much. You always seemed to be there when I really needed you, even if you weren't always there when I wanted you. You helped me see how to follow what God put on my heart. That has helped me learn how to walk with him. I wouldn't trade my life in him now for anything."

"Me neither," Laurie added. "But then what good are these institutions?"

"Maybe it keeps all of those caught up in religion so busy, they don't have the energy to infect the rest of the world with it," I offered with a smirk.

"That wouldn't be a bad use of it." John smiled with me, then quickly turned serious. "But I'm afraid it's a bit more mixed than that. As you say, good teaching can help plant seeds, and groups like this can help make connections between fellow travelers that God can use for years to come. But that isn't without a price. Over time institutions can even become abusive when the demand for conformity takes over. I always encourage people to run when that happens. But that doesn't discount the fact that some can be relatively healthy. Family dynamics of love and compassion will weave themselves amongst the institutional elements and some community will actually happen. Remember your early days at City Center?"

"I do!" Laurie brightened. "So it wasn't all bad?"

"No, not at all. In fact, in the first days of a new group forming the focus is usually on God, not the needs of the institution. But that usually fades over time as financial pressures and the desire for routine and order subverts the simplicity of following Jesus. Relationships grow stale in routine, and when the machinery siphons off so much energy just to keep it running, it grows increasingly irrelevant."

"Do you think that's how God looks at it?" I had noticed John glancing over my shoulder in the last few seconds, but didn't realize someone else had joined us. I turned to see Bryce standing behind me.

"How long have you been here?" I asked.

"I just walked up. I was on my way to the car when I saw you sitting here and wondered if this was the infamous John."

I told him it was and introduced them.

"May I join you?" he asked. "This is right where I'm struggling."

"Of course," John said with a smile.

"Jake and I have had some great times over the last couple of months. I love what God is doing in him," Bryce said.

"You do?"

"I only knew Jake from a distance years ago, but I found him condescending to people who didn't think like he did. Then I heard some rumors about his leaving City Center and not attending anywhere and I thought he'd become another bitter casualty of the ministry. Then a few months ago his name began to come up in conversations and I liked what I heard. That's when I called him, and when we met I was surprised. This was not the Jake I had known. So much had changed in him and the things he talked about stirred my deepest hungers.

"But the more I live this journey of life in Christ, the less motivated I am to keep up with all this," he said, motioning at the towering facility gleaming in the sun. "I'm not at all comfortable with the growth going on here. The more people we draw, the emptier we seem to become. This is a great place to hide—to come regularly, even feel blessed. I keep telling myself we're doing some wonderful things here, which keeps me going. But in my honest moments, I question all that. I would certainly walk away if God thinks it as irrelevant as you said a minute ago."

"Please understand that I didn't mean you are irrelevant to God or that these people are. They're not. By 'irrelevant' I meant that God looks past the institution and deals with people. He wants them to know him and experience real community with one another. He'll keep inviting them into that their whole lives."

"So you don't have a problem with my speaking here, John?" I asked, a bit relieved.

"Of course not, Jake. I have no problem going wherever God goes and he certainly will be here drawing people to himself."

Bryce continued, "But for all the work that goes on here and all the money we spend, the resulting spiritual fruit is pretty meager. New people aren't coming to know God. Our new people are transfers from other congregations that are having trouble. I don't know anyone here who is on the journey Jake is, and only a few who share my hunger, and we're so busy we don't do much about it." Bryce's voice cracked as the struggle I'd seen so often in him surfaced.

John reached out to cover Bryce's hand with his own. "It can't be other than it is. Once people are in love with the program and grow dependent on it as the spiritual component of their lives, they won't see its limitations. It cannot substitute for their own life in him and it can only produce an illusion of community because it is based on people doing what it takes to sustain the institution."

"But couldn't it be better? I'm torn between the responsibility to reform it and the desire to leave it. Neither sounds like a good option. I doubt it can be reformed, or at least that I can do it. I already have some people questioning my leadership when I talk about my struggles. And I have no idea how I'd make a living if I walked away."

John just let his words hang in the air for a moment, as did I. I knew this was the seminal question that Bryce struggled with. I had no answer for him and I was dying to know what John might say. As we waited, I noticed another flock of geese over John's shoulder, calling out as they joined the other flocks moving south.

"What should I do? Is it evil and should I run from it? Can it be better if guys like Jake stayed around as counterbalancing voices to those who want to serve the machine?" He looked at me with a smile. We'd had this discussion before. He'd even asked once if I would consider coming on his staff.

"People have been trying to reform it for two thousand years, and the result is almost always the same—a new system emerges to replace the old, but it eventually becomes a substitute of its own. Have you noticed that those who share your hunger don't share your passion to reform the machinery?"

"I have noticed that. The people whose spiritual maturity I respect most seem to gravitate away from helping us run this thing. I've been very disappointed that they won't join our leadership teams. It means we have people in leadership positions who don't know God very well, but who have strong opinions about the way things should be done."

"That should tell you something."

"It tells me that maybe the ones I thought were mature aren't, since they were so unwilling to serve us."

"Okay, that's one possibility, or maybe they wanted to invest their time serving people instead of attending an endless supply of committee meetings."

"I was afraid of that one," Bryce said, letting a frustrated smile peek out. "But that leaves the machinery, as you call it, to people who don't know God's character. They are impossible to work with."

"That's a problem, isn't it? Structures are about gaining power and getting your own way. Those who are growing to know him don't need them."

"And there are moments I'm not sure whether I want to use my talents to keep it going if it is not effective for the kingdom, especially if it robs my family of a dad because I'm gone all the time."

"Is that how it feels?"

"Not to me, but my wife says that's how it is. She may be right. I'll admit to being so drawn into all the activity here at a human level that I don't notice stuff like that."

"You'd do well to listen to her, but more important, listen to Jesus. Bryce, it seems to me you're trying to make a decision about your future based on principle instead of simple obedience. Is Jesus asking you to be here, or is he asking you to leave it?"

"I was hoping you'd give me some criteria that would make it easier to know."

"And rob you of the chance to hear him breathe his will into your own heart?" John answered with a gracious smile. "Never. This is between you and him. Sorting it out with him will help your relationship grow. Don't look for a right or wrong answer to what you're asking. Then you have to condemn others who don't choose what you do. He may want you to stay longer, to love these people and let your hunger encourage them."

"Or frustrate them," Bryce corrected.

"It does do both." John smiled. "Or he may want you to walk away and watch him take care of you in ways you will never learn here. I have no idea which it is."

"That's where I'm stuck. I just don't know. On any given day I vacillate wildly depending on the circumstance I'm in."

"That's why it would help to get your eyes off the circumstances and look to him. He can take you through anything and perfect his purpose in you as he does it."

"I just don't know," Bryce said, shaking his head. "Maybe I'm just afraid of losing my income."

"Are you?" John asked.

"I wouldn't be honest if I said I don't think about it. I trained for this. I don't know if I'm qualified for much else."

"You'd be surprised what Father might ask you to do and how he might resource you. But all you can do is take that fear to him and ask him to show you the way."

"I have. A thousand times," Bryce said with a sigh.

"Then it isn't time," I found myself saying to my own surprise, and out of the corner of my eye I saw John smile and subtly nod.

"What does that mean, Jake?"

"Part of the journey involves doing what he makes clear to you. If you've submitted it to him, then let him sort it out. If he were asking you to leave today, I think you'd know that, even in the face of your fears. If he hasn't made it clear to you, then wait. Just keep loving him and following him every day. I'm learning the joy of resting in him, doing what I know to do and not doing what I don't know to do. It's been one of the hardest lessons to learn, but also the most freeing."

"But I want a right or wrong answer." Bryce's frustration was bleeding through.

"Don't we all," I said, appreciating his frustration, "until he becomes answer enough? This is his decision, not yours, and it will be clear when it is clear."

"Just ask him whom he wants you to be walking with right now," John offered. "Don't try to sort out what you want or what you think is best. Follow the growing conviction he settles in your heart over time."

"This may not even be your decision. Someone else may get to decide it for you," I added.

"He often works that way, too," John agreed.

"How so?"

"I didn't choose to leave City Center. I got fired, remember?"

"That does sound like fun." Bryce's voice dripped with sarcasm.

"Jake's right," John spoke up. "Sometimes we don't know what God wants because there are stories yet to play out and people's lives still to be impacted by yours."

"So it really is a day-to-day walk, letting Jesus sort out his way in us?" Bryce said.

"Yes, it is, Bryce, and when you learn to live that way you'll never want to go back. Jesus is really good at showing you how to do it, especially when your desire to please him is not competing with doing what you think is best or easiest."

"Like putting my financial security above my spiritual passion," Bryce mumbled more to himself than the rest of us.

"That's probably the hardest one. They don't call it the 'Puritan work ethic' for nothing." John smiled.

"I have so much invested here, John. I don't know if I could walk away if I knew that's what he was asking."

"You're right, you don't know. You'll be surprised what you'll do when the way is clear. Someday you might just have more valuable things to do than what you're doing here."

"So what am I supposed to do about all of this in the meantime?"

"Keep following your hunger. Be honest about it with yourself. Do each day what he puts in your heart to do."

"What if that creates some real conflict?"

"Such as?"

"I don't know. I'm already starting to hear some rumblings because I'm not hyping the offering enough or pressuring people more into helping with children's church. When I encourage people to rely on God, my associate thinks I'm just neglecting my job."

"Believe me, I know," John answered with a measure of sorrow in his voice. "But you need to follow Jesus, even when it creates conflict. Always be gentle and gracious to everyone, but never compromise what is in your heart just to get along. I have no idea how this will all play out for you, but it always does, in ways we can't imagine."

"But I could get killed this way."

"Yes, you could. But if you're going to follow him, what choice do you have? Follow the hunger, Bryce. It will continue to shape you and give you courage for whatever lies ahead."

"If I end up leaving, should I tell others to leave, too?"

"Why, what would that help?"

"To save them from all of this and point them to something more real."

"Pointing them to Jesus is always helpful. Telling people to leave rarely is. What if Jake had told you to do that five years ago?"

"I would have thought him a divisive rebel and wouldn't have had anything to do with him."

"How would that have helped you? It would have only made you more resistant to what God has done in you in the five years since."

Bryce was deep in thought now.

"You see, Bryce, truth has its time. If you tell someone the truth before they're ready to hear it, you can push them further away, no matter how well intentioned you might be."

"How do I know they aren't ready?"

"Do you really think hundreds of people will be ready, on the same day, some Sunday morning?" John was smiling and Bryce soon joined him.

"I get that, but what about individuals?"

"You have to let Jesus show you. He can help you sense when people are ready and when you need to hold back. Make sure you really have their best interests in mind—that you are not using them to validate your own choice by pushing them to agree with you. That never works. Also, listen to the questions people are asking and it will help you know if they're hungry for more. Even with Jake, I've put nuggets out there and watched to see what he did with them. If he listened, struggled, and asked more, I took him further. If he didn't, I let it go! I was trying to serve him. I didn't need to validate myself."

I was surprised at his answer, and I wondered what I had missed because I hadn't caught where he was going. It made me wonder if this was why Jesus spoke in parables and metaphors—to help hungry people see without unnecessarily hardening those who were not ready. I'd have to explore that more.

"I guess the bottom line is that if I want to find an expression of church life that fulfills what the Scriptures talk about, I either have to change this organization or leave it."

"Or stop looking for it."

"What? Are you serious?"

"No institutional arrangement will ever contain all that the church is. Don't look for it institutionally. Look for it relationally. Certainly the New Testament talks about the priorities of that church—Jesus as its sole head and focus, daily encouragement among believers, plural and lateral leadership, open participation, and an environment of freedom so people can grow in him."

"Like what I have with Jake?"

"And there will be others God will give you as you simply follow him," John added. "Some will help you for a time on your journey and others you will help on theirs, but mostly you will find yourself mutually sharing his life together."

"But if we structured around that passion . . ." Bryce's voice faded away as he tried to figure out how to finish that sentence. Finally his head cocked to one side. "Are structure and passion polar opposites?"

"No, they're not. Not all structure is wrong. Simple structures that facilitate sharing his life together can be incredibly positive. The problem comes when structures take on lives of their own and provide substitutes for our dependence upon Jesus."

"So I don't need to look for the perfect church or try to put one together?"

"The way you mean that, I'd say no. But Jesus is putting together a church without spot or wrinkle. It includes everyone in this community and around the world who live in a growing relationship with him. It's okay for you to look at how that church expresses itself every day in the people and events around you. Just don't try to corral it into something you control. It just won't work. Jesus saw the church as a reality, not an assignment for his followers to construct. She is growing, all around you. You just can't see it now because your focal point is far short of her beauty and immensity."

"How can I change that?"

"There's only one way—stay focused on him. Where Jesus is given first place, the church simply emerges in wonderful ways. He will place you in the body exactly as he desires. And as those relationships grow, you may find yourself surrounded by a group of people who want to walk in a more intentional community together. That's an amazing thing when it happens, but still you have to keep your focus on him. Even groups that start out centered on him are easily and quickly tempted to organize themselves to death. When Jesus ceases to be the object of our pursuit, our fellowship with his body will fade into emptiness."

"I don't know what to say." The struggle was evident on Bryce's face. "This goes against everything I've been taught. I've been trained to do this, to stay in control. I feel so powerless to live the way you're talking."

"That's how the system controls us." John shook his head in empathy. "It's a system we think we can work through our own initiative and effort, but that is also why it cannot produce the life you hunger for. That's only found in him."

"And only when I give up control."

"Or the illusion of it, Bryce," I said. "The hardest-won lesson of this journey is that I was never in control. I only thought I was."

John sat quietly, so I continued. "Real community is not something we fabricate by any means. It is a gift God gives."

"But doesn't that directly conflict with most of what I do here?"

"Does it?" John asked.

"I'm wondering that. Oh, we're generous about it. We don't overtly manipulate people, but nothing we do directly encourages people to live this kind of life. We talk about it, we want people to do it, but our efforts are geared to the growth and success of this institution. We're not teaching them to depend on him in any practical way but to find their security in being part of what we do."

"Maybe it's time to live it differently," John suggested.

Bryce sat quietly for a moment. "I know the best we can produce falls far short of the life I watch Jake living. We call singing together 'worship' and regular attendance 'fellowship,' and we've convinced ourselves we're actually doing those things just by coming, whether they're real in our hearts or not. We've taught people to be committed to our services and programs and let them think that doing so validates them."

"Whether or not they are really coming to know him," I said.

"That's it! I've had a greater depth of fellowship with you, Jake, in the last two months than with anyone I have known here for years. With you I can be honest about my hungers and not feel judged. Here people seem to be looking for ulterior motives."

"The freedom to be honest and the freedom to struggle are key to a real friendship," John said.

"Here we've tried to do it as an obligation for believers. We tell people to be committed to our gatherings and to one of our small groups."

*Wow, I remember thinking that way in what seems like a lifetime ago.* "I did, too," I admitted. "But I see that differently today. How could obligation ever produce real relationship, Bryce? Obligations are only necessary when the experience is ineffective or lifeless. When people are living in the life of Jesus, they will treasure every opportunity to connect with other brothers and sisters who are also on this journey. It will not be something they *have* to do, but something they wouldn't ever want to live without."

"It always comes back to that, doesn't it? If we're seeking to live in him, these other things sort out. If we're not, no matter what else we do it will always fall short of our hungers."

"Absolutely. He is the impetus that brings us together, and without that no commitment will suffice." As I was talking it was becoming far clearer to me than I had thought it through before. "I'm becoming convinced that the church Jesus is building transcends every human approach we've tried to use to replicate or contain it."

"You mean there isn't some way that we can gather as God's people that fulfills the hope of the New Testament church?"

"Oh, there's a gathering that does that," John said with a certainty that took me by surprise.

"Really? I'd like to hear about it," I said.

Just then another flock of squawking geese flew over the trees and drew all our eyes skyward and held our gaze as the ever-shifting V headed southward.

"They get it!" John said with a smile as we all looked back down.

"Get what?"

"There's a gathering going on. They are all headed south to warmer weather. It's not so important what group they're with at the moment, but that they're headed in the right direction."

"So we should all fly south?" Bryce asked, clueless as to what John was talking about.

"You think of gatherings as meetings to go to and trying to craft the perfect format that will guarantee results that no meeting can guarantee. But you don't see yet that Jesus is always gathering his flock to himself. People from all over the world are finding their hunger for him eclipsing their hunger for anything else and that every substitute they try only adds to their restlessness. As they keep their eyes on him, not only do they grow closer to him with each passing day, but they find themselves alongside others who are headed that way, too. Geese fly together like that not because they are obligated to do so, but because it lightens their load and lifts them closer to their goal."

John turned his head skyward again and we joined him, now seeing at least four different flocks all heading south. "And all of those flocks will end up in the same place, together. That's all Jesus ever wanted—one flock drawn to him alone, and each helping lighten the load of others they find going the same direction as they are.

"That's the gathering. It's not when you meet, where you meet, or how you meet in meetings, but that you are gathering your heart to him. If that's happening, you usually won't find your-self going it alone very long. You'll find others heading the same direction, and by traveling together you'll be able to help one another along the way. That's why you only hurt yourself when you look for people who want to meet a certain way or think like you do about everything. Every person who crosses your path, believer or unbeliever, in an institution like this or outside of it, is a potential partner in this journey. By loving them to the degree that they allow, you'll participate in his great gathering.

"But the goal remains the same. It's him! It's always him—not a style of meeting or a preplanned program, not a safe salary, or a predictable future."

None of us said anything, though something clicked deep inside me. I knew what he was saying was far more impor-tant than I could grasp at the moment. We sat in silent reflection as we watched the birds fade into the horizon.

"I still don't know what to do," Bryce said, cracking a smile of feigned frustration.

"Yes, you do," John said, smirking back.

"I know." Bryce shook his head. "Follow him, every day! As scary as that sounds, there's a real freedom in it, isn't there?"

"That there is. And you'll do that best when you can relax in his working. He's not trying to make it difficult; he wants you to experience the very kingdom itself. This is his joy he draws you to, not some tiresome duty or empty promise."

With that, John's ride to Los Angeles pulled up in the parking lot. As he left, Bryce turned to me. "I see why you like him so much, Jake."

"I've not met anyone else like him."

"Neither have I, Jake, neither have I."

# 13

# The Final Parting

I saw his familiar form sitting on the bench where we had had our first conversation almost four years ago.

John had called me earlier that day and asked if I could meet him around six PM at the park where this whole journey began. Driving there I thought of all that John and I had been through over those years and smiled, grateful for his wisdom and compassion. Our relationship had certainly changed during that time. I had long since lost the desperate need to pepper him with questions and had come to simply enjoy his friendship. But what a friendship it was! I came away from every encounter with John feeling as if my trust in Father had grown tremendously.

I got out of my car, stepping into a spring breeze that swept across my face, bringing the sweet scent of citrus blossoms from a nearby orchard. As I walked toward John, he was in an animated conversation with a young man who seemed to be in the middle of his workout. He continued to jog in place while they talked. As I got closer, they shook hands with a smile and the jogger continued on his run. John jumped up from the bench to welcome me.

"Hi, Jake. Thanks for coming. I wanted to see you again before I left."

We hugged. "Before you left? You're always leaving."

"Fair enough." He smiled. "But not usually so far away."

"Really? Where are you going?"

"I'm going overseas for a while to visit some people in Africa, and I don't think I'll be back this way again. I wanted to touch base with you one more time."

My heart sank. I couldn't imagine he wouldn't be a permanent if infrequent fixture in my life. "I'm sorry to hear that," I said. "But my loss is certainly their gain. I'm sure they will be as blessed to know you as I have been."

"You didn't always feel that way."

It was easy to remember how frustrated John had made me in those early days. The more I listened to him, the more my life kept falling apart.

"Well, it wasn't easy at the beginning. You really got me into trouble."

"Oh, no I didn't. I never told you to do one thing. I simply made some observations, asked some questions, and gave you some options. The choices were all yours."

"I realize that, but they didn't always turn out so well."

"How could they? You had two desires that conflicted with one another."

"What do you mean?"

"You had this incredible hunger to know God and follow him. But you also wanted to be circumstantially secure and well liked by others. Those just aren't compatible with following him. We are safe because he is with us, not because our circumstances are easy, and trying to get everyone to like you only made you less a person than God made you to be. When you started following what God put in your heart, the other kingdom had to collapse. It was inevitable if not enviable. It is never easy watching people go through it."

"But those are good days to have behind me."

"That they are, Jake!" John said with a chuckle.

"I had no idea how real Jesus could be to me and my family. I had no idea how much of my thinking about following him was backward. I love the way things have sorted out. As painful as it all has been, I can truly say this is the life my heart has always been searching for. Even my best days inside of religion left me feeling a bit empty at times and always frustrated that I should be doing more and that God should, too. I don't have that now. Even on tough days I am grateful for what God is sorting out in me so that I can live more freely in him. There's not a night now that we go to bed when Laurie and I are not grateful for how God is working in us and the people he's put us in touch with."

"That's wonderful. Contentment is one of the best gifts on this journey."

"And yet it is more than that. Before, I was so focused on what I wanted from God and how I could get him to fulfill my desires. Now I just want to know him and let him change me so that his reflection can be seen in me. It's hard to explain. Before, I tried to act like a Christian. Now, I find myself doing and saying things that surprise even me. He's changed me, John, and I can't take any credit for it."

"That is as it should be, Jake."

"I am just sorry it took me so long to get this all sorted out."

"Time isn't Father's focus, Jake. He enjoys setting things right in us, even if it does take a bit of time. What you've learned now will never be stolen from you, no matter where God asks you to walk and whomever he asks you to walk alongside."

"This life in Christ is everything Laurie and I had ever hoped for, and yet none of it fits in the packages where we had always expected to find it. I had an incredible encounter yesterday, John, that leaves me in awe at the ways in which God works."

"What happened?"

"I had jury duty and I wasn't looking forward to it. While we waited in the assembly room, I was reading *Time* magazine. I was alone in a row of empty chairs when a young, beautiful woman walked up and sat down in the chair right next to me. I had no idea what she wanted but turned to greet her. She told me her name was Nicole. After a bit of small talk about our jobs, families, and frustrations with jury duty, I had no sense where the conversation was going so I turned back to my magazine.

"The next thing I know, she grabbed my arm. She began to cry and told me she thought her dad hated her. When I asked why, she told me about this horrible fight they had had the night before. As the details spilled out, it seemed to me she had misunderstood what her father was telling her. I could hear words I had said to my own children and knew I hadn't meant them the way she was taking them. I suggested that she might be misunderstanding her father.

"I tried to help her look at it from her father's perspective and she was surprised to think she might have gotten it all wrong. 'So you think my dad loves me?' she asked. I told her I didn't know him at all and only he could answer that, but it was worth finding out. She told me she would stop at her dad's house after she got out of jury duty to find out what he really meant."

"That's great," John said.

"That's not even the best part. A few minutes later she got called out for jury service. She gathered her things and stood up to follow the others to her courtroom. As she said good-bye, on an impulse I reached up to put my hand on hers and found myself asking her if she would answer a question for me. She nodded. 'How are things with your heavenly Dad?' I asked.

"You could tell she had no idea what I was talking about. Finally she asked if I was talking about God. I told her I was. I'll never forget her response as she almost snarled. 'I grew up with all that. I hate him.'

"I smiled at her and said, 'Nicole, as wrong as you might be about your earthly dad, you are dead wrong about your heavenly Dad. You have a Father who loves you more than anyone on this planet ever has or ever will.' As her face lit up with wonder, she asked me if it could really be true, and if it was, what she was supposed to do about it. She had to leave immediately, so all I could say to her was 'If I were you, when I walk out those doors, I'd say to God that if he was as loving as I just said he was, would he make himself known?' She assured me she would and left. I know God had his eye on her and it was fun to actually be part of a conversation like that and have no regrets afterward about the things I said or didn't say."

"The more at peace we are with ourselves, the easier it is for God to use us to touch others. What a fabulous story!"

"And it's not just me. There are so many others who are learning to live this journey with freedom and joy. Do you remember the home group you met with that evening?"

"I do, and I was going to ask you what had come of that."

"I'm not sure how to answer that. We still get together, though irregularly. It rarely looks like the meetings we used to have. We've learned to live more as a family and give time to the people God brings into our lives. My story with Nicole is just one of many that we are experiencing as God gives us away to others. Laurie and I have just started meeting with a group of new believers on Tuesday nights who wanted us to help them sort out their own relationship with God. They are some of the most enjoyable times we've ever had."

"And Bryce?"

"I don't know how that will work out yet. We're still getting together and having some great conversations. He's still growing, but he's caught between the real desire of his heart and the expectations others put on him. It's creating a bit of a division between those who share his hunger and those who are threatened by them. The next month or so will be crucial."

"You'll stay close to him?"

"Absolutely, though the road ahead won't be easy regardless of what happens."

"After all you've been through, I wouldn't be surprised if you ran from a situation like this."

"Part of me wants to. But there is no way I'd let him go through this alone."

Just then we noticed a rising tide of voices beginning to

spill into our conversation. We could sense the temper of them before we could hear their content. They were tense and angry. We both looked up to see nearly a dozen people heading our way carrying picnic coolers as their children were already scattering to play in the park. They were headed for the picnic pavilion tucked in the trees behind the bench where John and I were sitting. As they approached their words became clearer and we found ourselves caught in their conversation.

"If I have to sit through one more church service, I think I'll die."

"You and me both!" his friend responded.

"You'd better be careful with that kind of talk," one of the women offered.

"Or what? Is lightning going to strike?"

"No, but it may get back to Pastor and then you'll regret it."

"When I first came to this church, it seemed so alive and I felt like people really cared about one another. Now it's just one dose of guilt after another. We just can't seem to do enough for God. We're already out four nights a week with all that we're involved in. I'm exhausted. I have nothing more to give."

"Well, maybe he wasn't talking about you, then."

"No? Then why do I feel so guilty?"

"I don't know. He means well, and though he may not always get it right, he is God's anointed."

"If I hear that one more time . . ." one man started to say before he was interrupted.

The next words were so pained that I turned involuntarily to see where they were coming from. It was the smallest lady in their group. She had been quiet, but the words exploded out of her mouth as if a dam had burst. "God's anointed, my eye. He's out to build his own kingdom, and elders like you just sit by and let him do it. It's destroying me and my family and no one gives a rip."

Some of those surrounding her actually gasped, their mouths hanging open in stunned silence. The woman seemed shocked, too, by her own words. As soon as she realized what she had done, she buried her face in her hands and began to sob. Two women moved to console her. The rest stood frozen.

I looked back at John. His eyes were closed as if in prayer and he looked as if he was in pain. As he looked up at me, the briefest smile crossed his face. "Do you want to handle this, or do you want me to?"

"Handle what?" I asked, unsure what he was referring to.

John tilted his head toward the pavilion behind us and the awkward silence that hung over the group as a few of them began to open their coolers and pull out the food.

"We can't just butt in."

"At this moment I don't think they would see it as butting in," John said.

"You want me to talk to them?" I had a hard time imagining how that would happen.

"Well, I think it's for you to do, if you're up for it," John said with a smile. "I've got to be going anyway."

With that he stood up and I joined him. "Good-bye, Jake." He said it with such finality that tears welled up in my eyes.

"Will I see you again?"

"It's not likely," he said. "At least on this side of eternity."

"Thank you for everything you have done for me," I said, choking back my own tears. "I can't imagine how I would have survived all this if you hadn't been alongside."

"It wasn't me, Jake," John said, breaking the embrace and picking up a small duffel bag that had been lying under the bench. "It was Father all along, and he has many ways to do what he does."

"Just the same, I'm glad it was you."

"I'm also glad it was me. Now some others need your help, Jake, if you're willing," John said, nodding again toward the pavilion behind us.

"I'm willing, but I have no idea what to say."

"It will come to you. Just go and love them."

With that, John patted me on the shoulder and started off across the park. I watched him walk away and finally knew the answer to the question that had plagued me for so long. I knew who John was now and the answer was so incredibly simple. I shook my head with a knowing sigh.

Then I turned toward the picnic tables, still trying to think of what I could possibly say. At that moment one of the men pointed his finger at the woman who had exploded in pain. "You should be ashamed of yourself, Sally. Jesus would never talk like that."

That's when just the right words came to mind, something I'd heard a long time ago in what now seemed like another life.

I slipped in among their little group and, as gently as I could, I asked, "You really have no idea what Jesus is like, do you?"

And that began another conversation and a host of stories I don't have time to tell.

# About the Authors

**Wayne Jacobsen** wanders the world helping people sort out what Jesus really taught about life in his Father and in relational community with other believers. He is an author whose books and articles can be found at lifestream.org. He was a contributing editor to *Leadership Journal* for more than twenty years and also cohosts a weekly podcast at thegodjourney.com for those thinking outside the box of organized religion. He resides with his wife, Sara, in Moorpark, California, and can be contacted at:

Lifestream
www.lifestream.org
7228 University Drive • Moorpark, CA 93021
(805) 529-1728
waynej@lifestream.org

**Dave Coleman** has been a pastor and hospice chaplain but has most effectively lived his life as a brother helping others sort out the journey of life in Jesus. He has taught extensively on themes of marriage and living in God's grace and purpose, and he has worked as a volunteer in alcohol rehab. He lives in Visalia, California, with his wife, Donna. You can write Dave at:

dcoleman7070@att.net

# Appendix

## Why I Don't Go to Church Anymore!

by Wayne Jacobsen

*This article appeared in the May 2001 edition of BodyLife (www. lifestream.org) and has been passed around the world to give people a perspective and a vocabulary to help others understand how they can embrace life in the body of Christ in more relational ways than traditional congregational life often allows. This letter responds to those who would argue that you have to belong to a local institution to be part of the church.*

### Dear Fellow Believer,

I do appreciate your concern for me and your willingness to raise issues that have caused you concern. I know the way I relate to the church is a bit unconventional, and some even call it dangerous. Believe me, I understand that concern because I used to think that way myself, and I even taught others to as well.

If you are happy with the status quo of organized religion today, you may not like what you read here. My purpose is not to convince you to see this incredible church the same way I do but to answer your questions as openly and honestly as I can. Even if we don't end up agreeing, I hope you will understand that our differences need not estrange us as members of Christ's body.

### Where do you go to church?

I have never liked this question, even when I was able to answer it with a specific organization. I know what it means culturally, but it is based on a false premise—that church is something you can go to, as in a specific event, location, or organized group. I think Jesus looks at the church quite differently. He didn't talk about it as a place to go to, but a way of living in relationship with him and with other followers of his.

Asking me where I go to church is like asking me where I go to Jacobsen. How do I answer that? I am a Jacobsen, and where I go a Jacobsen is. "Church" is that kind of word. It doesn't identify a location or an institution. It describes a people and how they relate to one another. If we lose sight of that, our understanding of the church will be distorted and we'll miss out on much of its joy.

---

*He didn't talk about it as a place to go to, but a way of living in relationship with him and with other followers of his.*

---

### Are you just trying to avoid the question?

I know it may sound only like quibbling over words, but words are important. When we only ascribe the term "church" to week-end gatherings or institutions that have organized themselves as "churches," we miss out on what it means to live as Christ's body. It will give us a false sense of security to think that by attending a meeting once a week, we are participating in God's church.

Conversely, I hear people talk about "leaving the church" when they stop attending a specific congregation. But if the church is something we are, not someplace we go, how can we leave it unless we abandon Christ himself? And if I think only of a specific congregation as my part of the church, haven't I separated myself from a host of other brothers and sisters who do not attend the same one I do?

The idea that those who gather on Sunday mornings to watch a praise concert and listen to a teaching are part of the church and those who do not, are not, would be foreign to Jesus. The issue is not where we are at a given time during the weekend, but how we are living in him and with other believers all week long.

## But don't we need regular fellowship?

I wouldn't say we need it. If we were in a place where we couldn't find other believers, Jesus certainly would be able to take care of us. Thus, I'd phrase that a bit differently: will people who are growing to know the living God also desire real and meaningful connections with other believers? Absolutely! The call to the kingdom is not a call to isolation. All the people I've ever met who are thriving in the life of Jesus have a desire to share authentic fellowship with other believers. They realize that whatever they know of God's life is just in part, and only the fullest revelation of him is in the church.

But sometimes that kind of fellowship is not easy to find. Periodically on this journey we may go through times when we can't seem to find any other believers who share our hunger. That's especially true for those who find that conforming to the expectations of the religious institutions around them diminishes their relationship with Jesus. They may find themselves excluded by believers with whom they've shared close friendship. But no one going through that looks on that time as a treat. It is incredibly painful and they will look for other hungry believers to share the journey with.

My favorite expression of body life is where a local group of people chooses to walk together for a bit of the journey by cultivating close friendships and learning how to listen to God together.

## Shouldn't we be committed to a local fellowship?

That has been said so often today that most of us assume it is in the Bible somewhere. I haven't found it yet. Many of us have been led to believe that we can't possibly survive without the "covering of the body" and will either fall into error or backslide into sin. But doesn't that happen inside our local congregations as well?

I know many people who live outside those structures and find not only an ever-deepening relationship with God, but also connections with other believers that run far deeper than they found in the institution. I haven't lost any of my passion for Jesus or my affection for his church. If anything, those have grown by leaps and bounds in recent years.

Scripture does encourage us to be devoted to one another, not committed to an institution. Jesus indicated that whenever two or three people get together focused on him, they would experience the vitality of church life.

Is it helpful to regularly participate in a local expression of that reality? Of course. But we make a huge mistake when we assume that fellowship takes place just because we attend the same event together, even regularly, or because we belong to the same organization. Fellowship happens where people share the journey of knowing Jesus together. It consists of open, honest sharing, genuine concern about each other's spiritual well-being and encouragement for people to follow Jesus in whatever way he leads them.

### But don't our institutions keep us from error?

I'm sorry to burst your bubble here, but every major heresy that has been inflicted on God's people for the last two thousand years has come from organized groups with "leaders" who thought they knew God's mind better than anyone around them. Conversely, virtually every move of God among people hungering for him was rejected by the "church" of that day. The people were excluded, excommunicated, or executed for following God.

If that is where you hope to find security, I'm afraid it is sorely misplaced. Jesus didn't tell us that "going to church" would keep us safe but that trusting him would. He gave us an anointing of the Spirit so that we would know the difference between truth and error. That anointing is cultivated as we learn his ways in his Word and grow closer to his heart. It will help you recognize when expressions of church you share life with become destructive to his work in you.

### So are traditional congregations wrong?

Absolutely not! I have found many of them with people who love God and are seeking to grow in his ways. I visit a couple dozen different congregations a year that I find are far more centered on relationship than religion. Jesus is at the center of their life together, and those who act as leaders are true servants and are not playing the politics of leadership so that all are encouraged to minister to one another.

I pray that even more of them are renewed in a passion for Jesus, a genuine concern for one another, and a willingness to serve the world with God's love. But I think we'd have to admit that these are rare in our communities. Many last only for a short span before they unwittingly look to institutional answers for the needs of the body instead of remaining dependent on Jesus. When that happens, do not feel condemned if God leads you not to go along with them.

---

*Every person I've ever met who is thriving in the life of Jesus has a desire to share authentic fellowship with other believers.*

---

### So should I stop going to church, too?

I'm afraid that question also misses the point. You see, I don't believe you're going to church any more than I am. We're just part of it. Be your part, however Jesus calls you to and wherever he places you. Not all of us grow in the same environment.

If you gather with a group of believers at a specific time and place, and that participation helps you grow closer to Jesus and allows you to follow his work in you, by all means don't think you have to leave. Keep in mind, however, that of itself is not the church. It is just one of many expressions of it in the place where you live.

Don't be tricked into thinking that just because you attend its meetings you are experiencing real body life. That comes only as God connects you with a handful of brothers and sisters with whom you can build close friendships and share the real ups and downs of this journey.

That can happen among traditional congregations, as it can also happen beyond them. In the last seven years I've met hundreds if not thousands of people who have grown disillusioned with traditional congregations and are thriving spiritually as they share God's life with others, mostly in their homes.

### Then meeting in homes is the answer?

Of course not. But let's be clear: as fun as it is to enjoy large group worship and even be instructed by gifted teachers, the real joy of body life can't be shared in huge groups. For its first three hundred years, the church found the home the perfect place to gather. Homes are much more suited to the dynamics of family, which is how Jesus described his body.

But meeting in homes is no cure-all. I've been to some very sick home meetings and met in facilities with groups who shared an authentic body life together. But the time I spend in regular body life I want to spend face-to-face with a group of people. I know it isn't popular today, when people find it is far easier to sit through a finely tuned (or not so finely tuned) service and go home without ever having to open up their lives or care about another person's journey.

What matters most to me is not where or how they meet, but whether or not people are focused on Jesus and really helping one another on the journey to becoming like him. Meetings are less the issue here than the quality of relationships. I am always looking for people like that wherever I am and always rejoice when I find them. In our new home in Moorpark, we've found a few folks and are hopeful to find even more.

---

*It is far more important that our children experience real fellowship among believers than the bells and whistles of a slick children's program.*

---

### Aren't you just reacting out of hurt?

I suppose that is possible and time will tell, I guess, but I honestly don't believe so. Anyone who is engaged in real body life will get hurt at times. But there are two kinds of hurt. There's the kind of pain that points to a problem that can be fixed with the right care—such as a badly sprained ankle. Then there's the kind of pain that can only be fixed by pulling away—as when you put your hand on a hot stove.

Perhaps all of us have experienced some measure of pain as we have tried to fit God's life into institutions. For a long time most of us hung in there, hoping if we tweaked a few things it would get better.

Though we could be successful in limited ways during moments of renewal, we also discovered that eventually the conformity an institution demands and the freedom people need to grow in Christ are at odds with each other. It has happened with virtually every group formed throughout the history of Christianity.

### Are you looking for the perfect church?

No, and I don't anticipate finding one this side of eternity. Finding perfection is not my goal, but finding people with God's priorities is. It's one thing for people to struggle toward an ideal they share together. It's another to realize that our ideals have little in common.

I make no secret of the fact that I am deeply troubled by the state of organized Christianity. Most of what we call "church" today is nothing more than a well-planned performance with little actual connection between believers. Believers are encouraged toward a growing dependency on the system or its leadership rather than on Jesus himself. We spend more energy conforming behavior to what the institution needs rather than helping people be transformed at the foot of the cross!

I'm tired of trying to fellowship with people who view church only as a two-hour-a-week dumping ground for guilt while they live the rest of the week with the same priorities as the world. I'm tired of those who depend on their own works of righteousness but who have no compassion for the people of the world. I'm tired of insecure people using the body of Christ as an extension of their own egos and will manipulate the body to satisfy their own needs. I'm tired of sermons filled more with the bondage of religion than the freedom of God's love, and where relationships take a backseat to the demands of an efficient institution.

### But don't our children need church activities?

I'd suggest that what they need most is to be integrated into God's life through relational fellowship with other believers. Ninety-two percent of children who grow up in Sunday schools with all the puppets and high-powered entertainment leave "church" when they leave their parents' homes. Instead of filling our children with ethics and rules, we need to demonstrate how to live in God's life together.

Even sociologists tell us that the number one factor in determining whether a child will thrive in society is if they have deep, personal friendships with nonrelative adults. No Sunday school can fill that role. I know of one community in Australia that, after twenty years of sharing God's life together as families, could say that they had not lost one child from the faith as they grew into adulthood. I know I cut across the grain here, but it is far more important that our children experience real fellowship among believers than the bells and whistles of a slick children's program.

## What dynamics of body life do you look for?

I'm always looking for a people who are seeking to follow the living Christ. He is at the center of their lives, their affections, and their conversation. They look to be authentic and free others to hurt when they hurt, to question what they question, and to follow his voice without others accusing them of being divisive or rebellious. I look for people who are not wasting their money on extravagant buildings or flashy programs, where people sitting next to one another are not strangers, and where they all participate as a priesthood to God instead of watch passively from a safe distance.

## Aren't you giving people an excuse to sit home and do nothing?

I hope not, though I know it is a danger. I realize some people who leave traditional congregations end up abusing that freedom to satisfy their own desires and thus miss out on church life altogether. Neither am I a fan of "church hoppers," who whip around to one place after another, looking for the latest fad or the best opportunity to fulfill their own selfish desires.

But most of the people I meet and talk with are not outside the system because they have lost their passion for Jesus or his people, but only because the traditional congregations near them couldn't satisfy their hunger for relationship. They are seeking authentic expressions of body life and pay an incredible cost to seek it out. Believe me, we would all find it easier just to go with the flow, but once you've tasted living fellowship between passionate believers, it is impossible to settle for anything less.

### Isn't this view of church divisive?

Not of itself. People make it divisive when they demand that people conform to their revelation of truth. Most of us on the journey are accused of being divisive because freedom can be threatening to those who find their security in a religious system. But most of us aren't trying to recruit others to leave their congregations. We see the body of Christ as big enough to encompass God's people, in whatever way he calls them to gather.

One of the things often said about traditional church is that Sunday morning is the most segregated hour in American culture. We meet only with people who look like we do and like things the way we do. I've now found that I have far more opportunity to meet with people from a broader cross section of his body. I don't demand others do it my way, and I hope in time that those who see it differently will stop demanding we conform to theirs.

*In our day we don't need more talk about the church, we need people who are simply ready to live its reality.*

### Where can I find that kind of fellowship?

There's no easy answer here. It might be right in front of you among the fellowship you're already in. It might be down the street in your neighborhood or across a cubicle at work. You can also get involved in compassionate outreaches to the needy and broken in your locality as a way to live out his life in you and meet others with a similar hunger.

Don't expect this kind of fellowship to fall easily into an organization. It is organic, and Jesus can lead you to it right where you are. Look for him to put a dozen or so folks around your life with whom you can share the journey. They may not even all go to the same congregation you do. They might be neighbors or coworkers who are following God. Wouldn't that kind of interconnection among God's people yield some incredible fruit?

Don't expect it to be easy or run smoothly. It will take some specific choices on your part to be obedient to Jesus. It may take some training to shake off old habits and be free to let him build his community around you, but it is all worth it. I know it bothers some people that I don't take my regular place in a pew on Sunday morning, but I can tell you absolutely that my worst days outside organized religion are still better than my best days inside it. To me the difference is like listening to someone talk about golf or actually taking a set of clubs out to a course and playing golf. Being his church is like that. In our day we don't need more talk about the church, we need people who are simply ready to live its reality.

People all over the world are freshly discovering how to do that again. You can be one of them as you let him place you in his body as he desires.